Planning, Teaching and Class Management in Primary Schools

Second Edition

Planning, Teaching and Class Management in Primary Schools

Second Edition

Denis Hayes

 **David Fulton** Publishers

David Fulton Publishers Ltd
The Chiswick Centre, 414 Chiswick High Road, London W4 5TF

www.fultonpublishers.co.uk

David Fulton Publishers is a division of Granada Learning Limited, part of Granada Media plc.

First published in Great Britain by David Fulton Publishers 1999
Second edition published in 2003
10 9 8 7 6 5 4 3 2 1

British Library Cataloguing in Publication Data
A catalogue record for this book is available from the British Library.

ISBN 1–84312–018–6

Typeset by FiSH Books, London
Printed and bound in Scotland by Scotprint, Haddington

Contents

This book is dedicated to my wife, Margaret.

Preface

Learning to teach is exciting and challenging. Despite conflicting claims about effective policy, standards, parental rights, societal obligations and political aspirations, it is still the relationship between teacher and taught, the joy of discovering new things and the thrill of achievement which lie at the heart of education (Brighouse and Woods 2003). And regardless of the changes to the curriculum that have taken place over the years, the ability to plan, teach and manage children to give them the best possible chance of learning remains an essential element of the teacher's role.

It is sometimes difficult for inexperienced teachers and trainees to realise that previous status and hard-won accolades count for little when they meet a new group of children. Most pupils take only a passing interest in a teacher's past successes or failures; they are principally interested in finding answers to some key questions:

- Can this person teach?
- Can this person keep order?
- Is this person nice or nasty?
- Will this person be interesting and fun to be with?
- Can I trust this person?
- Is this person for me or against me?

Pupils may not express their thoughts in quite this way, of course, but they will quickly discover the answers to their unspoken questions through a variety of strategies which children have used down the years to test out new teachers, including calling out, innocent questions, sighs and depressed looks and feigned ignorance. Every teacher must be ready to counteract all such ploys by positive means, notably through careful lesson planning, enthusiastic teaching and a no-nonsense attitude. Perseverance, a willingness to learn from mistakes and determination are essential attributes for every aspiring teacher.

In addition, all novice teachers discover that what appears to come so easily to the experienced teacher is, in fact, extremely demanding and difficult to achieve and sustain...

- The class teacher calls for quiet and the children stop talking. The student teacher does the same thing and some children stop, while others continue. As the student is busy admonishing the disobedient ones, those who stopped talking re-commence their conversations.
- The class teacher prepares a worksheet for the lesson in a few minutes. The student attempts something similar and is up until late at night.
- The class teacher chats to parents at the door in a relaxed and personable way. The student tries to do the same and gets her words tangled.
- The class teacher marks some books and finishes them in half an hour, together with some helpful comments at the end of the page. The student takes three times as long and agonises over what to write.

These examples are not given to depress trainees but to reinforce the often overlooked axiom that teaching does not 'come naturally' to the majority of people. There are some students who seem to have an indefinable instinct for the job, but most have to battle and persevere with the challenges which inevitably arise in a situation where one adult has responsibility for the education of large numbers of pupils. All those who enter upon teaching must expect some hard times before reaping the rich rewards of a fulfilling career.

There is a lot more to being a teacher than planning, teaching and class management (see Cole 2002). There is the emotion attached to being a guest in someone else's classroom, working with children you have never met before and discovering the explicit and covert expectations of staff in the school. There is the anxiety to establish and maintain a good working relationship with the host teachers, especially the class teacher. There is the lurking suspicion that somehow you are not going to be good enough to cope or that you will be asked to take responsibilities before you are ready to handle them. Nothing that is written in a book can wholly prepare you for the multitude of decisions that face you in school, the demands of planning, the sense that there is never enough time to do everything, and the tension that arises when a tutor assesses your teaching. Nothing that is written can describe the pleasure of seeing a child understand something that was previously confusing, the trusting smile from a shy infant, or the animated enthusiasm from a junior aged child for whom the world is brimming over with hope and expectation. *Planning, Teaching and Class Management in Primary Schools* does not attempt to provide you with simplistic answers to complex issues. It does, however, offer important insights and strategies that can be used as a framework for monitoring and strengthening your progress as a teacher so that time on school placement becomes a first rate preparation for the day you have your own class.

Denis Hayes
Exmouth

Abbreviations

A	Assessment
AT	Attainment Target
CR	Critical Reflection
DfEE	Department for Education and Employment
DfES	Department for Education and Skills
EAL	English as an Additional Language
FPT	*Foundations of Primary Teaching* (Hayes 1999)
ICT	Information and Communication Technology
IEP	Individual Education Plan
KS	Key Stage
NQT	Newly Qualified Teacher
Ofsted	Office for Standards in Education
P	Planning
QCA	Qualifications and Curriculum Authority
QTS	Qualified Teacher Status
R	Reporting
SATs	Standard Assessment Tasks
SCAA	School Curriculum and Assessment Authority
SEN	Special Educational Needs
SENCO	Special Educational Needs Coordinator
TA	Teaching Approach
TMS	Teaching Methods and Strategies
TTA	Teacher Training Agency

Introduction

Planning, Teaching and Class Management in Primary Schools is divided into two parts. Part I examines general issues that relate to planning, teaching and class management at all levels. It is particularly intended to assist aspiring teachers, regardless of the point they have reached in their training, but will also be of interest to newly qualified teachers and teaching assistants who seek to understand better the principles and issues relating to classroom practice. The layout of Part I draws from the structure used in earlier competence documentation, notably DfEE 1998b.

Part II is built on information found in two publications by the Teacher Training Agency (TTA), namely, *Qualifying to Teach: Professional Standards for QTS and Requirements for Initial Teacher Training* (TTA 2002a) and the *Handbook of Guidance on QTS Standards and ITT Requirements* (TTA 2002b). Part II uses the standards' statements and suggestions in the *Handbook* as the starting point for a structured and accessible means of showing how competence can be recognised and ultimately achieved. The use of a range of case studies offers insights into the sorts of issues faced by trainee (student) teachers and confronts the realities of working in a classroom situation. Part II is particularly relevant to more experienced trainees who are looking towards qualified teacher status.

The standards that form the heart of this book can be used in a number of different ways (see Table 1). They refer to the competence that you should (ideally) achieve by the *end* of your training programme, so bear this truth in mind when evaluating your progress against the descriptions. It is also important to underline the fact that however rigid the standards' statements appear to be, they should be treated as beacons to guide your path rather than barriers to block your progress!

Table 1 Ways of using the standards statements

- As a basis for planning and curriculum continuity and development
- To write reflective commentaries or journals on the issues raised through the statements
- For students and tutors/mentors to agree a specific focus during classroom observation
- As a basis for a final assessment of student competence in planning, teaching and class management

PART I

Areas of Competence

Fragmeting a teacher's competence into discrete units does not reflect the complexity and dilemmas involved in the job but, for practical purposes, the different components are separately itemised so that you can focus on specific aspects of your planning, teaching and class management. Part I is set out for ease of use under seven chapter headings:

Chapter 1: Planning (*preparing lessons*)
Chapter 2: Teaching Approach (*the way that you go about your work*)
Chapter 3: Teaching Methods and Strategies (*the skills you employ*)
Chapter 4: Special Educational Needs (*ensuring that all abilities are catered for*)
Chapter 5: Assessment (*monitoring children's progress in learning*)
Chapter 6: Reporting (*communicating assessment information to others*)
Chapter 7: Critical Reflection (*closely considering your own practice*)

Each chapter consists of a number of sections, each of which has its own code. For example, the nine sections under 'Planning' are referred to using the letter P. Thus: P1, P2, P3, and so on. Similarly, the sections under 'Teaching Approach' use the prefix TA. Thus: TA1, TA2, TA3, etc. Throughout Part I of the book, there are a number of cross-references indicated to show major links between sections in different chapters.

Each section is laid out in the same way, starting with the identifying code, then the nature of the standard (based on DfEE 1998b), suggestions about the issues and practical factors that you need to take account of to meet the standard and a *Keynote* statement. For instance, under 'Teaching Methods and Strategies' (TMS), there are twelve sections, the first of which (TMS1) relates to the standard: *Use teaching methods which sustain the momentum of pupils' work and keep all pupils engaged.* For this particular standard, there follows six sub-sections explaining what you need to take account of, each of which has a Keynote statement attached.

In addition, at the end of each section, there is a *Competence check* with a summary of three key points for the standard.

The letters *FPT* in the text show that further information is available in Hayes (1999), *Foundations of Primary Teaching.*

Finally, it is essential to stress that the information contained in Part I is intended to provide a helpful framework of principles and ideas within which your creativity can flourish, and not as a dreary checklist of unattainable ideals to depress your spirits! Before going into school, you are advised to read straight through Part I and use the information as the basis for thinking, discussing and determining the implications for your classroom practice. Once you commence teaching, use the Competence check as a quick method for determining your progress, and the content of the sub-sections as the basis for evaluating the process of planning, teaching and class management in detail.

CHAPTER 1

Planning (P1–9)

Planning your lessons requires competence in nine key areas:

P1 What is taught.
P2 What teaching and assessment strategies are employed.
P3 What tasks are set to challenge and motivate pupils.
P4 How pupils' targets are set.
P5 How pupils with learning difficulties are dealt with.
P6 How lessons are structured.
P7 How continuity is provided between lessons.
P8 How a lesson incorporates the affective domain.
P9 How a lesson conforms to the National Curriculum programme.

P1 Identify clear and appropriate teaching objectives and content

What you need to take account of...

Terminology needs clarifying

Words such as 'aim', 'goal', 'objective', 'purpose' and 'intention' are liberally scattered throughout educational literature. Most commonly, the words 'aim' and 'goal' are concerned with final outcomes. The word 'objective' is most often used to describe the steps on the way to achieving the aim. For example, if the aim is learning to use a protractor, objectives may include an understanding about direction, the ability to employ appropriate terminology, an understanding of angular measurement, identifying, constructing and measuring angles using crude instruments, before finally using different types of protractor in problem solving or investigations. The words 'purpose' and 'intention' are used interchangeably as broad terms describing what a teacher hopes to achieve in the lesson with particular reference to children's learning. It is worth clarifying what you mean when you use terms and ensure that the tutor reading your lesson plan shares that view. In reality, pupils who appear to have succeeded in achieving the aim (target) on one occasion may still have only a tentative grasp of the subject area and require regular reminders and opportunity to rehearse and practise their skills.

Keynote: To use planning terminology consistently.

The main lesson purpose

If the lesson does not have a specific purpose it is difficult to know how to go about teaching it. You should be clear about whether the principal purpose is to extend pupils' knowledge, develop their conceptual understanding, practise skills or consolidate former learning. Even if it is a combination of some or all of these elements, it is worth clarifying this in your lesson plan by stating the intentions under the three headings: knowledge; concepts; skills. In broad terms, most of the knowledge will be provided by you through direct teaching or pupils finding out for themselves from books and databases. Most of the concepts will be developed through conversation, question-and-answer sessions and investigative play. Skills enhancement may take the form of consolidating knowledge and concepts through problem solving or improving ability through application to specific practical tasks.

Keynote: To be clear about the lesson purpose.

The likely learning patterns

In lesson preparation it is important to be clear not only about its purpose but about the way in which the purpose is to be realised. Some forms of learning can be mastered by means of following a well-defined sequence (such as using computer software); some learning takes place by means of overlapping stages in which a presentation of new ideas is necessarily preceded by reviewing earlier ones (such as in a science investigation); some forms of learning are more random and do not follow an obvious pattern (such as a problem-solving activity which can take one of many possible directions). Many lessons take the form of an initial teacher introduction, followed by set tasks and a conclusion, though note that if your introduction is only used to explain the tasks without improving pupils' understanding or sharpening their appetite for discovering more, an important opportunity for learning has been lost.

Keynote: To think about the way in which pupils learn best.

Mismatches between teaching objectives and learning outcomes

Lessons should be planned in such a way that the teaching approach helps to bring about particular learning outcomes. However, teachers cannot legislate for what children will learn and it is sometimes different from their original intentions. Sometimes, lessons take unexpected turns and the anticipated learning outcomes are not achieved. This can happen for many reasons, such as an interesting diversion due to a pupil's discovery, the posing of a thoughtful question or the re-interpretation of a task that provides for an exciting appraisal of existing methods. If the lesson involves a lot of direct-transmission teaching in which the teacher dominates the talk, the outcome is more predictable. If the lesson involves a lot of interaction between teacher and taught, especially if pupils are being encouraged to ask questions and pose problems, it is sometimes more difficult to predict outcomes, as conversations may take unexpected directions. Due to the unpredictable nature of learning, it is important to spend part of each lesson assessing (through what pupils say, write or do) the extent to which your teaching objectives have been matched by pupils' learning (see A1).

Keynote: To take account of the way in which teaching intentions may have to be modified.

Teaching about learning

There are occasions when the lesson content is less important than the process of learning. For instance, pupils may be involved in collaborative ventures or discussions where the purpose is primarily the development of social and interactive skills. Although the National Curriculum requires that pupils acquire specific skills and concepts, there are many occasions (such as structured play activities) when 'learning about learning' through social interaction is essential. Similarly, it is important for children to learn how to work independently without relying too much on their peers or an adult. Some children take time to gain the necessary skills and confidence to make their own decisions; others find it hard to take anybody else's opinions into account! You have to decide how much time to devote to activities which enhance the pupils' competence in collaborative and independent learning modes. It is rare that these skills can be accomplished in a hurry; nevertheless, part of your job is to help children to help themselves (see TMS9).

Keynote: To ensure that pupils have the necessary skills to complete tasks successfully.

Competence check

- ❏ I am clear about the main purpose of the lesson
- ❏ I have thought through the likely patterns of learning
- ❏ I have taken account of other learning that might take place

P2 Specify the teaching approaches and assessment strategies for achieving stated objectives

What you need to take account of...

Your intentions and children's capability

All teaching approaches must bear in mind what you want the children to learn and the abilities, speed of work and motivation of the children in the class. Planning lessons and taking account of teaching approaches needs to be guided by what pupils have achieved and are capable of achieving with your help. It is important to know what children already understand and what they have already experienced. Lessons cannot normally be planned in isolation from the classroom context in which they are to be taught if they are to be effective. If your lesson plans assume too little of pupils, they will become bored and restless; if they assume too much, you will spend most of the lesson reinforcing previous ideas which were never properly mastered.

Keynote: To know how far pupils are capable of progressing.

There are various teaching approaches

Different lessons require different approaches and assessment strategies. It is unwise to adopt a single approach – such as transmission teaching where you do most of the talking or group work in which you do little more than monitor progress – and claim that it 'works for me'. It is probable that your preferred approach is more appropriate to some circumstances than to others. For example, you may want to spend more time on explanation at the start of a new phase of learning than you do when pupils have grasped the basic principles and are spending time practising what they have been taught. Although you will want to reflect the class teacher's approach in your teaching and work hard to make a success of it, you should not be afraid to experiment with different methods. It is important to visit other classes to widen your experience and see the variety of methods used.

Keynote: To utilise a range of teaching approaches appropriate to the situation.

Greater differentiation requires more involved preparation

Lessons in which every child does more or less the same work will require less differentiation and matching of task than lessons in which a range of learning needs have been catered for through different activities. However, the time required to plan, prepare and present differentiated learning tasks may be considerable. There are a number of ways of approaching the process of matching lesson content to ability. First, in the introductory phase of the lesson, you have to decide whether it is better to address the whole class at the same time about the lesson or speak to each group separately if they are doing different work. If you choose the latter, the children waiting for your attention must have a worthwhile 'holding task' until you become available. Second, the tasks must reflect the children's ability in terms of the vocabulary used, the concepts involved and the difficulty of the activity. Third, the final phase of a lesson increases in complexity in direct proportion to the range of different activities taking place. For instance, it is easier to conclude a lesson in which all the groups are dealing with computation exercises than it is if one group is doing maths, another problem solving and another art work.

Keynote: To ensure that the teaching and tasks are appropriate and manageable.

The overall teaching approach should incorporate a variety of methods

A teaching approach should be sufficiently flexible to allow for variation throughout the course of a lesson. For instance, the lesson may begin with a rehearsal of previously covered points, assessing pupils' understanding through a question-and-answer session, introducing the new material through demonstration and exposition, further question and answer to check understanding and extend pupils' thinking, allocating tasks, monitoring work on an individual or group basis, briefly reviewing the lesson with the whole class, and summarising key concepts or facilitating reporting-back from groups (see TMS5 and 6). Your own role in this unfolding lesson will depend on how much you want children to listen to you (or to one another), how much you want them to persevere with tasks and how much time you want to spend in determining what they have learned. For instance, on some occasions you will be teaching directly, on other occasions (such as hearing children's explanations about their work) you will be listening, and on others (such as when you are observing children at work without intervening) you will be assessing their understanding.

Keynote: To build a repertoire of methods.

Formative and summative assessment are both important

Assessment for every lesson should concentrate on the ongoing work as well as the anticipated end product. If you attempt to develop lessons that are too complex, you will not have the time to monitor pupils' progress and will have to rely on your summative assessments after the conclusion of the session when you mark work or check answers. Formative assessment takes place as you note children's responses, listen to their conversations, discuss their problems with them and examine their written output. It takes place so that you can offer advice, state an opinion about work, explain new possibilities or show that something is wrong (Clarke 2001). In order to do any of these things you have first had to monitor the situation, weigh up the possibilities and intervene as appropriate. Summative assessment has to wait until the task is completed or a natural juncture has been reached in the work whereby an evaluation of present progress can be carried out. It is important that you are clear about the school's marking policy when making a summative assessment (see *FPT*, Chapter 10).

Keynote: To use formative and summative assessment strategies effectively.

Assessment relies on a range of factors

Assessment should take account of the pupils' previous experience, the amount of help they received in completing the task and the level of difficulty they experienced in completing the task. You must also accept the possibility that pupils' progress has been hindered by your poor explanations, inappropriate match of task with ability, or failure to motivate and encourage their determined efforts. Where possible, involve pupils in evaluating the quality of their own work by allowing them to explain what they have done and why. Assessment is only useful if it assists the pupil's understanding, promotes a keener interest in the work and is accompanied by appropriate support in the form of advice, guidance or explanation. It is also important to take note of what pupils' achievements might tell you about your own teaching methods and effectiveness.

Keynote: To take account of all the facts before drawing conclusions.

Assessment requires careful judgement

Some assessment can be carried out through a formal test in which children provide answers to set questions; for example, during end of key stage assessments (SATs) and schools' internal monitoring procedures (see A4). Your own assessment of their progress must rely heavily upon regular scrutiny of their written and visual output, and verbal exchanges with them about aspects of the work, including question and answer. These two approaches (written/visual output; verbal exchanges) are less straightforward than they seem. Written outputs cannot always be taken at face value as some children find difficulty in recording things that they understand perfectly well. Children's answers to teachers' questions are often cloaked with embarrassment, fear about being wrong and inexperience in expressing themselves (see TA5 and TMS7). Your assessments will be more effective once you have gained the pupils' trust and understand them as learners, so be patient.

Keynote: To use the appropriate assessment technique.

Competence check

- ❏ I am sufficiently clear about my teaching approach
- ❏ I have taken the pupils' differing abilities into account in my planning
- ❏ I have a clear idea about how I will assess the success of my lesson

P3 Set tasks, including homework, which challenge and motivate pupils

What you need to take account of...

Tasks and activities serve a variety of purposes

Although the words 'task' and 'activity' tend to be used interchangeably, it is useful to think of a task as work with clearly defined parameters that have been established by the teacher, within which children must operate. An activity, on the other hand, has its roots in the word 'active' and allows for a more experiential approach involving problem solving, enquiry or investigation in which children work alone or (more often) collaborate to reach a solution. If you set a single task it must allow for the ability range that exists within the group or class and give each child opportunity to engage with the content, by either staging the task or setting different tasks for different abilities. If you stage the task, it should begin with a straightforward element with which all children can cope and gradually become more demanding. If you set separate tasks you must allow for the additional organisation and monitoring that this involves. Activities are more difficult to plan for in as much as the direction that the children will take is less predictable but the best type of activity allows all children to work at their own pace and contribute to a joint effort at their own level. However, bear in mind that an exploratory activity is not a free-for-all and is most productive when the children have been given (a) appropriate skills training, (b) clearly stated aims, (c) starting points to give them ideas about the general direction to take, (d) a framework within which to operate. Creativity flourishes in a secure and properly controlled environment, where children understand the constraints, have access to adequate resources and are purposefully focused. You may be surprised how much they can achieve!

Tasks are not a substitute for active teaching

Although investigative and problem-solving tasks help to secure understanding, extend thinking and enhance collaboration, they should not be seen as a substitute for direct, interactive classroom teaching which emanates from your own subject knowledge and ability to convey information in a relevant, persuasive manner. Children gain the most from experiential learning (through play or exploratory activities) when you have been instrumental in ensuring that they already have a strong knowledge base and appropriate skills. In the same way, setting homework which requires a level of skill and understanding that has not been previously nurtured in school will result in frustration and a lot of hard work the following morning as anxious children (and, perhaps, parents) flood you with questions about how to complete the tasks successfully.

Keynote: To set tasks which build on existing foundations.

Challenge comes in many forms

A task may be challenging due to its conceptual difficulty, the level of skill required to carry it out or the length of time it takes to complete it. Challenging classroom work should be invigorating and inspiring rather than disheartening and repressing. Challenges should stretch the children's thinking but not prove insurmountable. If you set homework that makes unreasonable demands upon children, it will prove to be counterproductive and may result in complaints from parents.

Keynote: To set tasks which allow all children to find success.

Pupil involvement in creating tasks is important

Some of the best challenges emerge from the children's own ideas and initiative. Their enthusiasm for pursuing learning will often be the spur for achieving effective outcomes. The highest levels of motivation occur when pupils are interested in what they are doing and believe that it is time well spent. However, even if you feel that you cannot rely on the children's ideas, you can sometimes offer them a choice from a limited menu of things that can usefully be done. The same homework does not have to apply to every child regardless of ability or aptitude; indeed, having a range of useful ongoing homework projects from which pupils can select over a period of time (days, weeks, half a term) often sit easily alongside more immediate ones. Parental involvement in homework is also more likely if the child shows genuine enthusiasm rather than grumpy subjection!

Keynote: To incorporate pupils' interests where possible.

Homework should not be an afterthought

Lesson planning should, where possible, include some reference to homework tasks. Although some teachers simply ask children to 'finish off the work', this is not always desirable as faster workers have little to do and slower (possibly more conscientious) workers have too much to complete. Homework should help to reinforce the day's work, allow opportunity for extending the pupils' knowledge or stimulate their thinking (Ofsted 1995). It is useful to have a broad homework plan for the month ahead which can be changed if necessary but provides a structure for continuity. Note that some schools have specific homework tasks which have to be administered in much the same way as any other part of the curriculum programme. If this is the case, introduce the tasks with the same enthusiasm and vitality that you would use were they your own choice.

Keynote: To consider homework as part of lesson planning.

Homework places additional demands upon teachers

Homework should be easily resourced and, wherever possible, self-assessed. Thirty pupils handing in thirty pieces of additional written work for marking and monitoring is a heavy burden to add to your existing workload. If you seek to involve parents in homework tasks, they will be keenly interested to know how highly their children achieved. This is sometimes due to the fact that some parents become so closely involved in the homework that they feel personally responsible for it (see TMS10). If homework is to succeed in helping children to learn more effectively, it has to take account of both logistical and parent-related factors.

Keynote: To keep homework tasks manageable for pupils and teachers.

Competence check

- ❑ My lessons provide a good foundation for extending learning
- ❑ I have considered pupils' ideas and suggestions when setting homework tasks
- ❑ The homework I have set is useful and appropriate

P4 Build on prior attainment to set clear targets for learning

What you need to take account of...

It takes time to establish what children already know

Although the requirement to discover what children already know sounds simple enough, it takes time and perseverance. Class records offer some information but talking to the class teacher is the best way of finding out about individual children. A test score also gives some indication of ability but says little about qualities such as perseverance, cooperation and speed of work. The most direct method for finding out what children know and understand is through talking to them, asking questions and putting them in problem-solving situations where they have to draw on their existing knowledge. However, you need to be aware that some children do not know what they know! That is, although the knowledge is buried just beneath the surface, they do not possess the necessary communicative ability to transmit it to an adult (especially someone they do not know well). A number of shy children will conceal their understanding due to fear of getting things wrong or lacking the confidence to tackle more demanding tasks. If you are only in the school for a small number of weeks, it will take time before you get the full measure of a class and know the children well enough to set them appropriate work. This is part of your learning process.

Keynote: To take nothing for granted.

There are different forms of learning

Some lessons allow for specific learning outcomes; others are to do with attitude, collaborative skills and exposure to ideas in advance of gaining a full grasp of concepts. Learning may have to do with facts (such as multiplication tables) or uncertainties (such as where responsibility lies for wars). It may involve exposure to new ideas or consolidating older ones. Learning may require a specific skill (such as knowing how to shape a clay pot) or draw upon a range of skills (such as in science problem-solving situations). Pupils have to learn social skills (such as not interrupting when someone is speaking) and understand procedures (such as how to operate a computer). Some learning comes through being told directly; others through playing, experimenting or simply messing about. It is important for you to bear in mind that different forms of learning require different amounts of lesson time; thus, whereas telling pupils something may take moments, allowing them to discover things for themselves may require hours. On the other hand, telling them may result in only temporary grasp of the facts, while self-discovery generates more enthusiasm and secure knowledge if accompanied by appropriate adult intervention and explanation. Your lesson plans must take account of the nature of learning and the practicalities of implementation.

Keynote: To be clear about the characteristics of different forms of learning.

Learning is never linear

Some children forget completely things they have learned; others require reminding; yet others never knew in the first place! It is difficult to distinguish children who did not grasp concepts during earlier lessons from those who had a tentative grasp but have lost some of their hold upon it. Learning is more cyclical than linear. It needs to be revisited from different directions before it is firmly rooted. It is also well known for some children to 'jump' a section of learning and master more difficult material while struggling with (apparently) more elementary ideas. Although the expression 'prior attainment' has a safe ring to it, all teachers discover that learning is a difficult term to define and even harder to demonstrate. Your lesson planning has to make some assumptions about children's prior attainment or you would never be able to plan anything. On the other hand, regular checking and monitoring of progress through question and answer and observation of the way that pupils deal with set work, will give you insight into whether learning is superficial or deeply embedded.

Keynote: To use various sources of evidence to assess the quality of learning.

Systematic teaching does not guarantee systematic learning

Building on prior attainment is not like setting a row of bricks upon one already laid; it is more like placing sticks on the glowing embers of a fire. You can prepare the most elaborate plans which respond to children's needs and take account of prior learning, organise and manage your lesson with great aplomb, yet find that some children have failed to grasp what you are teaching and require a variety of other approaches (sometimes less orthodox) to achieve the desired learning outcomes. Every lesson will consist of desirable learning intentions (those things that you hope that the children learn) and learning outcomes (those things that, in reality, they do learn). Sometimes the gap between intentions and outcomes is wider than is ideal. However, you can be sure that although some children will not learn exactly what you intended, they will learn things that you never intended, too.

Keynote: To be systematic in planning without being rigid.

You can take careful aim but discover a moving target

It is, of course, important to know what you are doing and why you are doing it, but it is foolish to set specific targets for learning which do not take account of changing circumstances and different contexts. If opportunities occur during a lesson to address important issues which were not in your original plan, it is normally worthwhile seizing them. Targets for learning cannot always be determined in advance; they often emerge as the lesson unfolds and the level of children's understanding becomes more apparent. A pre-lesson learning intention is not an immovable object; clues that you gain throughout the lesson about children's grasp of vocabulary, concepts, skills and the ability to apply them may significantly influence the time that you spend on a particular aspect of the lesson or the direction that you take. Lesson plans should not, therefore, be pursued irrespective of whether pupils understand what is happening. Although it takes a lot of courage and confidence to alter the direction of a lesson part way through, it is better than pursuing an inappropriate goal. For instance, you may discover that children do not possess the dextral skills that you anticipated and you will have to allow more time for them to practise; you might expect that they can complete a set task more quickly than they are able to and thereby have to postpone the lesson summary; you may find that a lot of children are making similar mistakes and have to stop the class while you repeat the explanation. If you are in the early stages of training and only have one chance to complete the lesson, you simply have to make the best of it. Gradually, you will improve your timing and expectations by paying careful attention to children's grasp of things as the lesson unfolds.

Keynote: To aim, fire and re-direct as appropriate.

Competence check

- ❑ I am sufficiently aware of what pupils already know and what they have already experienced
- ❑ My teaching is well structured, yet flexible
- ❑ I have realistic targets for pupil achievements

P5 Identify and respond appropriately to pupils with learning difficulties

What you need to take account of...

Learning difficulties are widespread

The majority of children have difficulty in learning certain skills or concepts. Even the most able children struggle from time to time, albeit at a higher conceptual level than less able pupils. Learning difficulties are not confined to core subjects. Some pupils struggle with rhythm in music lessons, orientation in map work, time sequences in history, designs in technology. Although the need to be able to read and write accurately and confidently is a priority, it is wrong to label children as having learning difficulties when they struggle in these areas without also acknowledging their expertise in other, less exposed aspects of learning. Similarly, it is rarely the case that academically able children are good at everything. Children may be perfectly capable of learning but have temporary difficulties due to factors such as bereavement, friendship issues or anxiety. Lesson planning cannot possibly take every factor into account but it pays to make a habit of looking out for pupils' uncertainties and misunderstandings across the spectrum of curriculum areas and keep brief notes about anything significant. Your lesson plans should take account of the need to remediate uncertainties through revising and reinforcing without losing sight of introducing fresh material. It is also important to distinguish between pupils who have a genuine lack of understanding and those who cannot be bothered to make the effort.

Keynote: To take account of pupils' lack of knowledge and misunderstanding in lesson planning and delivery.

There are short-term and long-term difficulties

Some learning difficulties are simply temporary blockages which require a slightly different emphasis in teaching approach or perseverance before they are removed; others are more chronic and seem to defy all attempts to help. Planning can take account of short-term problems through specific teaching for the group of children concerned; more deep-seated difficulties require longer-term strategies which may involve the school's special educational needs coordinator (SENCO; see SEN1). As a student on school placement, you can only play a small part in helping to rectify the longer-term problems by being aware of the individual education plans drawn up for individuals and taking account of their difficulties in your daily interaction with the class.

Keynote: To distinguish between temporary and chronic learning difficulties.

Pupils may have superficial or deep-seated learning difficulties

Learning difficulties range from broad ones such as 'generally weak at spelling' to particular ones such as regularly misspelling 'ie' and 'ei' words; the former is indicative of a deeply rooted problem requiring some targetted support, the latter can be dealt with by focused methods and deliberate targetting of problem words. Superficial learning difficulties can often be combated through intensive (and, if possible, enjoyable) teaching, together with additional homework and the support of parents. It is important that children who are struggling with superficial problems do not label themselves as failures in the subject (see TA5). For instance, children who misspell a few common words may start to call themselves 'useless' at spelling and gradually begin to convince themselves that it is true. Part of your job is to help children get things in perspective. You can help to enhance the positive classroom climate by adopting a 'you can do it' approach and helping pupils to gain in self-belief by offering them achievable short-term targets (Wassermann 1990).

Keynote: To diagnose the difficulty correctly.

Teachers cannot solve every learning difficulty by themselves

If the problems are severe, an appropriate response is to enlist the help of a more experienced member of staff; it is not necessary or desirable to try to deal with everything yourself. Some teachers have a 'learning difficulty' when it comes to enlisting help from colleagues! If you are a student, your class teacher will already be familiar with the scale of the problem and inform you accordingly. If a child has special needs (see SEN1), parents will sometimes be involved. Learning difficulties are not normally a sign of your failure or of the child's so it is helpful to see them as challenges rather than problems. There is support available from senior teachers and the SENCO, so there is no need to struggle on unaided.

Keynote: To use all available expertise.

Learning difficulties have different origins

Some learning difficulties are due to the amount of time the pupil takes to gain understanding or mastery. For instance, some able children may be slow to grasp something but ultimately prove to have a more thorough understanding than those who achieved immediate success. It is unwise to jump to conclusions about a child's ability. Although some learning difficulties in basic skills stand out clearly, others take time to detect. Many children are also able to conceal their shortcomings by using a variety of strategies (see TA5). Learning difficulties may reside in the individual child, the nature of the task or the way you teach it. Some children may be experiencing difficulties outside school, and although there is some uncertainty about the impact that social conditions have upon children's ability to learn, every teacher knows that contented, happy children are more likely to achieve their potential than those who are unsettled.

Keynote: To take account of factors underlying learning difficulties.

Competence check

- ❑ I have a clear idea of individuals' specific learning difficulties
- ❑ I have taken account of these difficulties in my lesson planning
- ❑ I am drawing on suitable advice to help me cope with the demands made by individuals' learning needs

P6 Provide a clear structure for individual lessons

What you need to take account of...

There is no such thing as an isolated lesson

A lesson should always link with what has gone before, while bearing in mind what lies ahead. Individual lessons are a convenient way of organising learning, but in reality learning takes place continuously at home and at school. If you are an inexperienced student, you may have to teach an isolated lesson as a means of practising lesson planning and class management, but it would be wrong to imagine that learning can be confined within a single lesson plan.

Keynote: To view individual lessons within an overall framework.

A clear structure is not the same as a rigid one

The lesson structure needs to be clear to you before it can be made clear to the pupils. You cannot hope to explain to pupils if you have not thought it through for yourself. Careful lesson preparation takes account of the likely order of events, the time that each phase of the lesson will take, the resources required, and the desired learning outcomes. Nevertheless, a lesson can take an unexpected twist for many reasons, including:

- the need to spend longer than anticipated on the revision section;
- children's responses to your questions or issues evoked as a result of their own questions;
- the length of time they take to complete the tasks;
- your awareness from monitoring the children's work that there is a widespread misunderstanding of something basic which requires immediate explanation;
- a general lack of motivation and enthusiasm. It takes a high level of professional judgement to decide when to persevere with the lesson formula that you so carefully prepared beforehand and when to deviate or even (in rare cases) abandon what you are doing.

Keynote: To be so well prepared that change can be accommodated.

The pupils are not privy to the teacher's thought processes

You may have spent a lot of time planning your lesson, but the pupils will be hearing about it for the first time. This necessitates a clear, firm and well-paced explanation rather than a hurried one. You should offer pupils the opportunity to ask questions about the tasks and your expectations for what they have to achieve (see TMS11). Pupils' questions range from basic ones which are for reassurance (so don't get cross if you have just told them that very thing!) to those which introduce creative ideas. Make your explanations pithy and convincing. Anticipate likely questions and have your answers ready.

Keynote: To let pupils know what is happening and what is expected of them.

Perfect preparation for every lesson is an ideal

Teaching, learning and assessment belong together. Your teaching should normally be accompanied by an indication of learning intentions and how you will monitor and assess the pupils' progress. However, no matter how well prepared you try to be, there will be occasions when you enter the classroom in a state of unpreparedness. At such times, the structure for your lesson should be as straightforward as possible. Sets of printed activities or text books can be invaluable as a short-term expedient. Experienced teachers sometimes rely on previous teaching occasions to bale them out of unprepared situations; students do not have that luxury.

Keynote: To strive for perfection while recognising reality.

Competence check

❏ My lesson preparation is orderly and comprehensive
❏ There is continuity between my present lesson and previous lessons
❏ The lesson purpose is clear to myself and the pupils

P7 Provide a clear structure for sequences of lessons

What you need to take account of...

Every lesson is related to another lesson or lessons

Children learn from lessons in the same subject but also draw on other learning from areas which lie outside the immediate one. Such links are referred to as 'cross-curricular' and allow for the transfer of knowledge, skills and understanding between subjects (see P9). The more that you can refer to ideas and concepts established through other subjects, the more pupils will conceive of learning as a whole rather than fragmented parts. Phrases such as 'do you remember how... ?' and 'think back to the other day when...' are useful spurs to establishing links.

Keynote: To exploit cross-curricular opportunities.

Lesson plans must be accommodated within the framework of curriculum planning

The longer the sequence of lessons, the less it is possible to write a lot of detail in advance. The school's medium-term plans offer a helpful framework, but the detail has to wait for the regular curriculum planning meetings between staff in the same subject area or age phase. Only then can your individual lesson plans be fully developed. The development of lesson plans must, therefore, take account of overall curriculum planning. In addition, no amount of pre-planning can allow for circumstances that may emerge over the time period of the lessons, so some modifications are inevitable.

Keynote: To see where lesson plans fit within the overall planning scheme.

Learning intentions should be considered before tasks and activities

A clear sequence of lessons must principally take account of the intended learning aims and objectives rather than activities to be done during those lessons. The activities should reinforce, develop and extend learning rather than act as a substitute. Lesson intentions can be gradually specified and linked with tasks and activities (see Figure 1). Bear in mind, however, that some learning emerges through activities such as play, problem solving and investigative work, not all of which can be predicted. Resourcing implications should be considered as the more free-flowing investigative activities may be curtailed due to lack of equipment or materials. Lesson plans can usefully be subdivided into three broad sections dealing with intentions, activities and resources.

Keynote: To consider intentions, then activities, then resources.

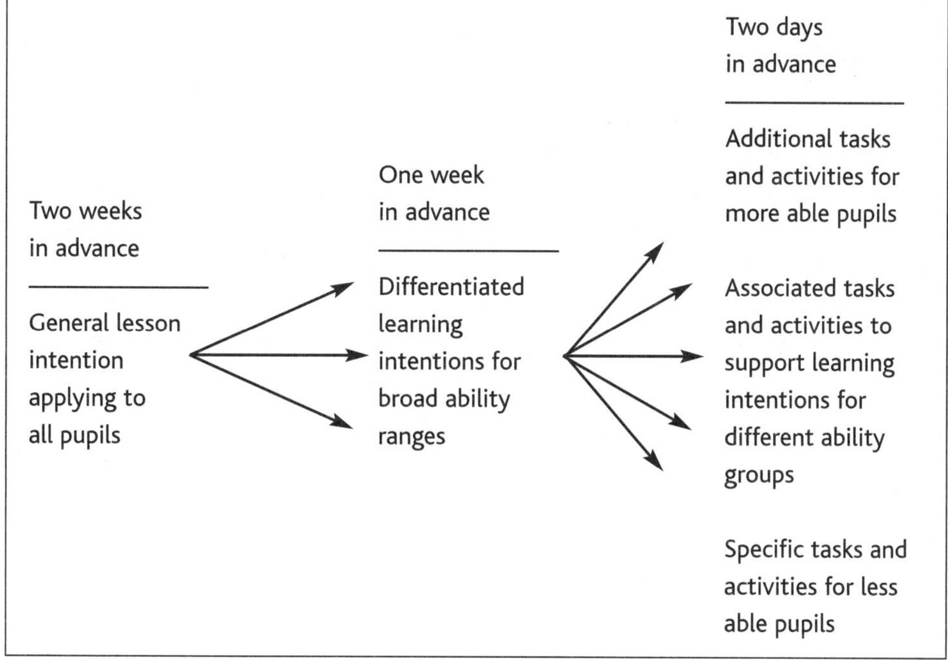

Figure 1 Increasing specificity in the planning process

Lesson sequences are subject to constraints

The danger of producing too many detailed lessons too far in advance is that they cannot take account of individual needs, the pace of learning and specific factors influencing the children's learning over time. Sequences of lessons (which are, after all, only strings of individual lessons) still need to take account of the differentiated learning needs of the whole class (McNamara and Moreton 1997). In practice, this requires a series of parallel learning intentions running through the series of lessons, something which is extremely difficult to maintain. A more practical approach to lesson sequencing is to have skeleton plans which can apply to the majority of children in the group or class and make more detailed plans nearer the time as the special needs and requirements become more apparent.

Keynote: To make advance plans which can be modified nearer the time.

Lesson sequencing is part of a rolling programme

Although many teachers plan for a half term, it is important to be constantly looking ahead and trying to predict possible trends and learning opportunities. For instance, an educational visit may be approaching which requires a special lesson focus; SATs tests, sports days or preparation for an assembly may involve disproportionately large chunks of time being devoted to that particular item. The availability of resources such as library packs and museum items may also influence the pattern of lesson arrangements. Sequences based on the National Curriculum programmes of study offer useful guidelines but cannot take account of individual school or classroom situations. Each subject area requires some element of advance planning and many lesson sequences can be based on the long-term curriculum programme; nevertheless, overlaps between subjects are both inevitable and desirable. Although it is important to draw up lesson plans in advance to provide a framework within which you can develop sufficient detail nearer the time, the need to look ahead requires constant vigilance.

Keynote: To take account of the unfolding patterns of school life.

Competence check

❑ I know exactly what I am doing this week
❑ I have a reasonable idea about the format of next week's lessons
❑ I have an outline framework for succeeding weeks' lessons

P8 Plan opportunities to contribute to pupils' personal, spiritual, moral, social and cultural development (PSMSC)

What you need to take account of to...

Development is influenced by teacher-pupil relationships

Plans for PSMSC developments are not only located in a lesson plan; they are embedded within teacher-pupil relationships. Many studies have shown that pupils are more likely to learn effectively when working with a teacher whom they admire and respect. Pupils do not like teachers who are sarcastic, embittered or mean; neither do they think much of those who are poorly prepared and introduce uninspiring lessons in an unenthusiastic manner. Your life and conduct provides the single most significant influence for the pupils in their school experience. If your pupils admire and respect you, they will be influenced by your opinions (Cooper and McIntyre 1995; Inman and Buck 1995). This is both a joy and a responsibility.

Keynote: To live out what we say.

Spontaneous opportunities may be significant

Opportunities for development exist within the planned and unplanned curriculum. Sometimes an older pupil's spontaneous, searching question can provide the basis for powerful discussions and provocative debate. Younger pupils can ask questions or make statements that are profoundly simple, thereby causing a lot of soul searching about fundamental truths. It is important to be as honest as possible, including acknowledging when you are uncertain, but be careful not to become trapped in conversations which are slightly unwholesome or unduly controversial. It is also quite easy to waste valuable lesson time talking about interesting but largely unimportant issues.

Keynote: To make good use of unplanned opportunities.

Personal development is individual

Personal development is largely about the kind of people we are: our actions, words, behaviour and maturity. There has been a considerable emphasis in recent years upon the rights of the individual. Your task is to acknowledge those rights but to inculcate a sense of personal responsibility, too. This can start in small ways in the classroom by promoting pride in its appearance, courtesy and caring, and allocating specific responsibilities to every pupil. As you value all children and their opinions (Suschitzky and Chapman 1998), you will also need to think carefully about helping them become more community orientated and good citizens. For example, children might be responsible for tidying one another's trays or be made a class monitor. A table-top inspection, involving every child in the group, with a recognised reward for the best (such as a small shield or flag) can encourage a sense of personal and corporate responsibility within the class. Lesson plans should be produced with affective as well as cognitive outcomes in mind.

Keynote: To promote rights and responsibilities.

Spiritual development touches the unseen

Spiritual development is concerned with dimensions of life which go beyond the immediate and visible, and provides a basis for pupils to clarify their views about life's meaning and its ultimate purpose. Some teachers claim that they have nothing to offer towards spiritual development as they 'do not have a faith' but this reticence is misplaced. We all believe something, even if it cannot be expressed using conventional spiritual terminology. The children in our care will be receiving a wide range of different messages from parents, friends, the media and religious groups about the deeper issues of existence and eternity. As their teacher, we have to help them make sense of what they hear at their own level of understanding. Every child can be led to appreciate the beauty of the natural world and be encouraged to see the worth of people they meet. All children feel the emotions of love and hate, and struggle with questions about why things happen, injustice and disappointment. You cannot impose your own perceptions and beliefs upon your pupils, but through structured sessions and informal opportunities you can help them to come to terms with difficult issues and feel more secure in a world where contradictory messages about the purpose of life abound.

Keynote: To help pupils to see that their lives have meaning and purpose.

Moral development deals principally with right and wrong

Moral development is concerned with forms of behaviour, attitudes to others and the rules of conduct which govern them. Moral norms have been challenged in recent years by those who claim that the only morality that counts is the one that is right for the individual concerned. As teacher, you first need to be clear about what you believe before you can help children to find their way through the moral maze. Although it is unwise to see yourself as an arbitrator in all things moral, you can uphold and promote fairness, respect, responsibility and compassion as central to the survival of every race and culture. If you are asked by children what you think about controversial issues, think hard before you answer; it is usually better to re-state your beliefs about basic principles of justice and harmony than to find yourself confronted by an angry parent wanting to know why you are leading the children astray with your outlandish views! The pupils in your class may not know precisely the difference between right and wrong, but they soon detect hypocrisy.

Keynote: To explore moral issues openly.

Social development is about our place in society

Social development is concerned with understanding the conventions of daily life and the structures which contribute towards good order and conduct. Pupils need to appreciate that community well-being depends upon intelligent conformity to social conventions. Some children come from backgrounds in which the conventions differ markedly from those in school. This presents particular difficulty for new entrants who often struggle with the contradictions between home and school. If you are a student working in someone else's classroom, you must familiarise yourself with the procedures, rituals and patterns of behaviour that the teacher has established, and try to maintain and strengthen them (Jones and Charlton 1996). If you are a newly qualified teacher, you need to establish your own rules as quickly as possible (see Table 2). Every lesson offers opportunities to enhance social development. It's all a matter of staying alert to them and using your influence to promote well-being.

Keynote: To foster an inclusive learning environment.

Table 2 Establishing classroom conventions and procedures

Conventions and procedures need to be established in the following areas:

- conversation
- possessions
- movement around the room
- movement outside the room
- taking turns
- choosing
- team games
- volume of talk
- manners
- relating to adults
- care of equipment
- choosing partners
- the production of drafts and practice pieces
- the quality of final products
- dealing with finished work
- sharpening pencils
- going to the toilet

Cultural development is about the way that communities behave

Cultural development is concerned with how groups in society behave and relate to one another and to those outside the community. Pupils need to acknowledge and respect cultural diversity, while celebrating aspects of their own heritage. Children from minority communities are likely to have specific home influences which impinge directly upon their behaviour and attitudes. The school will have policies relating to religious adherence, such as what may be worn and when absence is tolerated. Children whose parents adopt unusual lifestyles and expect schools to accept whatever they decide may find themselves torn between wanting to support their family traditions yet not wishing to be marked out as 'different' by their peers. Sometimes tensions between customs and school rules can create problems for children and teachers in determining what is acceptable. Nevertheless, antisocial behaviour cannot be tolerated and instances of it should be reported to your supervisor or senior colleague. Lesson planning must be sensitive to the effect that cultural diversity might bring – both the constraints and opportunities.

Keynote: To take account of cultural diversity.

Development is a process not a product

Some teachers become discouraged if their pupils do not become the sorts of people they hoped for. In your work with children, it is important to remember that you are just one factor in the tapestry of influences which constitute their experience. Although your role is important and may transform lives or at least make a substantial difference to children's attitudes and priorities, the final outcome rests largely with family and personal inclination. Your lesson planning and delivery should help to inform, provoke and stimulate an active interrogation of the issues, but never to indoctrinate. It should also recognise that learning is lifelong. Many people who achieve modestly at school gain success later on because of a teacher's encouragement.

Keynote: To do the best for each child.

Competence check

- ❏ I am developing sound relationships with my pupils
- ❏ I am sufficiently clear about the different developmental patterns
- ❏ There is consistency between my curriculum programme and my own attitudes and behaviour

P9 Ensure coverage of the appropriate programmes of study

What you need to take account of...

Some parts of the curriculum are optional and others essential

There is more flexibility in teaching history, geography, and design and technology than there is in teaching the core subjects of English, science, mathematics and information and communication technology (ICT). The core curriculum is formally assessed through national tests and therefore requires systematic teaching. Consequently, reading and numeracy should normally receive at least one hour's curriculum time per day. ICT is playing an increasingly important role in curriculum development and many schools have devoted considerable sums of money to ensuring that every child is computer literate. It is now a requirement that all student teachers possess a thorough grasp of how ICT is used in the classroom.

Keynote: To ensure that curriculum priorities are met.

Coverage needs to be consistent across classes

Teams of teachers (teaching the same year group, for instance) have to move through the curriculum at approximately the same pace. Fortnightly team meetings are often used for such monitoring. Consistency is not, of course, identical to 'sameness'. Content coverage simply ensures that when all the children from the same age phase move up to their next classes, none will be disadvantaged by missing important learning opportunities. Your own enthusiasm and commitment to teaching should not, of course, be constrained by conformity but you need to keep a close eye on what other teachers are doing.

Keynote: To keep in step with other teachers.

Coverage does not necessarily equate with learning

The coverage of the curriculum does not guarantee that children have learned from it. Although teachers are required to follow the programmes of study, some areas need more thorough treatment; others can be dealt with relatively easily. For instance, the concept of time is a difficult one for many young children; older pupils often struggle with the procedures associated with long division. You will find that a greater proportion of teacher-led instruction and teaching 'from the front' results in faster coverage but does not guarantee effectiveness. Some learning cannot be hurried and needs a combination of direct teaching, practice, discussion and regular revision. In your records of pupils' progress it is easy to tick the 'have met' column after covering a curriculum area but much more challenging to know when to tick the 'met and understood' column to indicate pupils' grasp of subject knowledge and the implications of what they have learned.

Keynote: To discriminate between curriculum coverage and learning.

Cross-curricular opportunities must not be overlooked

Coverage is not only confined to working through a list of topics in single subject areas such as maths and English, but of seeing the potential for overlap and the place of cross-curricular elements, such as through problem-solving activities, and the use of information technology. The more that children can see the links between areas of knowledge, the more they will perceive learning as a whole. Details of cross-curricular skills, themes and dimensions are listed in Table 3.

Keynote: To weave cross-curricular threads.

Table 3 Cross-curricular skills, themes and dimensions

Skills
These should be transferable and content free. Important ones include:

- communication
- numeracy
- study skills
- problem solving
- personal and social education
- information technology

Themes
There are five themes:

- economic and industrial understanding
- careers education and guidance
- health education
- education for citizenship
- environmental education

Dimensions
Based on the principle of equal opportunities and life in a multicultural society. Central principles involve the need for pupils:

- to be prepared for life in a multicultural world
- to fulfil their potential
- to have equal access to the curriculum
  and for teachers:
- to avoid making unwarranted assumptions about children
- to safeguard equal opportunities

Competence check

- ❑ I am familiar with the relevant programmes of study
- ❑ I know what has to be taught
- ❑ I am focusing on pupil learning more than coverage of curriculum programmes

CHAPTER 2

Teaching Approach (TA1–6)

You must demonstrate competence in six areas of teaching:

TA1 Teaching of individuals, groups and the whole class.
TA2 Using teaching time.
TA3 Monitoring progress and intervening in pupils' work.
TA4 Establishing and maintaining a working environment.
TA5 Ensuring pupils' safety and confidence.
TA6 Ensuring pupils' acquisition of knowledge, skills and understanding.

TA1 Effectively teach whole classes, groups and individuals

What you need to take account of...

There is a difference between efficient and effective teaching

Effective teaching should not be confused with efficient teaching. Effective teaching is largely concerned with product; efficient teaching with process. Effective teaching means that expectations are achieved or exceeded. Efficient teaching means that whereas the technical process of teaching is acceptably good, the learning intentions may or may not be achieved (Hayes *et al.* 2000).

Keynote: To aim for effectiveness through efficiency.

What it means to teach the whole class effectively

There are two ways in which to think of whole class teaching. First, when all the children are working on a broadly similar task or listening to, or interacting with the teacher at the same time. Second, when the teacher is responsible overall for all the children but the groups are involved in a variety of tasks/activities, possibly supervised by other adults. Consequently, you need to be clear about whether you are teaching the whole class as a single undifferentiated unit or whether you are responsible for a whole class which is divided up in particular ways (in collaborative groups, for instance) to achieve the desired outcomes. Effective whole-class teaching, especially when you are leading from the front, demands varied and engaging speech, interactive dialogue with the children through interesting questions, speculation and analogy, and the use of appropriate visual aids and board work. Interactive class teaching is a challenge for any teacher and requires a considerable degree of confidence and practice.

Keynote: To involve the whole class in learning.

What it means to teach groups effectively

Group work takes many forms. Grouping can be for the purpose of organisation when all pupils are sitting in random groups, working independently. It can be based on academic ability, friendship, class control factors (such as separating troublesome children) or using a mixture for collaborative activities when diversity can be helpful. Groups may work on similar tasks with the expectation being that some groups will work more slowly or less successfully than others; or on different tasks which take account of the speed and ability of the members of the groups. Whatever system of grouping you or the class teacher employ, it is important to be clear about why you have selected that option and how you will keep abreast of the demands that too much diversity places upon teachers in the classroom. Monitoring the progress of several groups, especially if they are involved in different types of task, is extremely difficult. It is best to keep your organising as straightforward as possible, especially in the early stages of working with the class. In all work with a group or groups you should ensure that:

(a) Tasks and activities allow the children to work unaided for part of the lesson.
(b) All members of a group have opportunity to participate in cooperative venture.
(c) You encourage mutual (peer) support whereby children share expertise, ideas and understanding.

It is particularly important to make it clear when children should be actively working together and when they should be working individually. Collaboration inevitably means an increase in noise level as the children talk together, so you have to make some allowance and encourage them to speak quietly without losing the spontaneity of active discussion. In doing so, avoid making comments 'into the air', like: 'It is far too noisy in here' (a statement of fact), but rather: 'Please speak in a hushed voice when you discuss the work' (a directive that can be monitored).

Keynote: To group pupils in such a way that it benefits their learning.

What it means to teach individuals effectively

The final repository for all learning is in the mind and heart of the individual child. Whatever strategies you use to secure the learning, the main proof of your teaching effectiveness is the impact upon the individual. There are occasions when you can spend quality time with one child but these are rare and precious moments; for the most part, children learn alongside their peers and have to glean whatever they can as a member of a group or whole class. One useful way of checking that children understand or can do something is to ask them to explain or demonstrate to their peers.

Keynote: To consider the learning needs of individuals.

Teaching intentions need to be realistic

In order to meet all teaching intentions for the whole class, group and individuals, the number of objectives must be reduced and sharpened. Your teaching will need to be decisive and focused. Too much curriculum task diversity places heavy demands upon your planning and organisation time beforehand, and your management and monitoring skills during the lesson. Student teachers and new teachers normally find that it is wise to restrict each lesson to a single curriculum area unless there is sufficient adult support available to allow for diversity.

Instead of trying to achieve too much in a single session, it is better to be thorough and check that children have gained a complete grasp and understanding of the lesson content by allowing them the time and opportunity to think about the ideas and issues being addressed. Mere coverage of content does not ensure understanding. The more closely you link assessment criteria with learning objectives, the easier it is to monitor whether your teaching is achieving the desired effect.

Keynote: To organise for learning in a manageable way.

Competence check

- ❏ My lesson plan clarifies the different teaching approaches I intend to adopt throughout the session
- ❏ I am focusing on effectiveness as well as efficiency
- ❏ I have taken account of the way in which individuals learn

TA2 Meet teaching objectives through effective use of teaching time

What you need to take account of...

There are many different time constraints

Making the best use of the available teaching time requires that you consider:

- the time that is formally available according to the timetable;
- other demands upon children's time such as movement between locations, longer than expected assemblies, play rehearsals, outings, and so forth;
- the time spent on lessons, which may not equate with learning, as the most memorable learning experiences are sometimes short and dramatic;
- the teaching time used for specific teaching of literacy and numeracy.

Although time constraints can be problematic, they can also help you to sharpen your organisation and set yourself targets for completion and achievement.

Keynote: To be sensitive to time factors.

There is a danger of confusing 'busyness' with learning

Using too much direct teaching without the necessary fallow times necessary for reflection, thinking, re-consideration and the raising of questions is counterproductive. You should develop opportunities for pupils to give 'yes but' responses and, where appropriate, probe complex ideas rather than passively accept them. There is, however, a need to be careful about random exploratory activities which use up a lot of time but achieve little, and convoluted problem-solving activities which substitute for well-constructed experiments. Although prospective parents visiting a school may be impressed by a quiet class, heads down, concentrating on the work in hand, a closer inspection of the learning taking place might show that there is more froth than substance.

Keynote: To use learning time effectively.

Time can be wasted through inadequate preparation and poor classroom organisation

Tasks such as sorting out groups and setting out resources should be organised beforehand wherever possible to save wasting valuable lesson time doing it. If pupils are left hanging around while you fiddle and scramble around to sort things out, the lesson gets off to a poor start which may be difficult to retrieve. There is no substitute for thorough preparation as a means of ensuring that the lesson goes well (Mackinnon 2002). It is essential to think through every stage of the lesson and anticipate possible problems and opportunities, such as children who have to attend other lessons part-way through, interruptions for watching TV programmes and the act of distributing resources. Time, tide and restless children wait for no one (Arnold 1990).

Keynote: To prepare well and organise in advance.

Time can be wasted through the use of inappropriate teaching methods

If a direct-teaching approach can achieve the same results as exploratory methods, it makes sense to use it. On the other hand, if a concept or skill needs to be practised and absorbed, there is little point in merely telling pupils when they need to experience it for themselves. Some teachers spend time unnecessarily in asking pupils low-level questions or asking them to 'read my mind', going from one child to another in an attempt to find one person who knows the correct answer. Although questioning technique is a powerful means of promoting thinking and stimulating ideas, it should be used alongside imaginative transmission teaching (see TMS6). Similarly, a lot of teachers have a habit of spending too long talking without involving their pupils; consequently, the time and energy expended results in limited learning as bored children gaze ahead vacantly or exhibit restless behaviour.

Keynote: To use appropriate teaching methods.

Teaching time can be affected by non-teaching responsibilities

Your duties do not end at the classroom door. There are meetings to attend, playground and bus duties to assist with, parents to speak to, telephone calls to make. There are colleagues to contact, tutors to inform, resources to gather and children to advise. All these factors influence your ability to prepare for sessions, get to classes in good time and mentally adjust to the demands of the classroom. Teaching time cannot be isolated from the teacher's wider professional responsibilities; nevertheless, you must try and ensure that teaching time is protected and used as effectively as possible. It is interesting to note that about half of a teacher's working week is spent in dealing with non-teaching tasks.

Keynote: To take account of the wide variety of duties and responsibilities.

Competence check

- ❑ I have taken account of time factors in my lesson planning
- ❑ I have organised my teaching in such a way as to avoid time wastage
- ❑ I am aware of other ways in which time might evaporate

TA3 Monitor and intervene when teaching to promote effective learning

What you need to take account of...

Knowing how to monitor and when to intervene requires considerable skill and professional judgement

Monitoring and intervention are concerned with both behaviour and learning, though the two are often related. Inexperienced teachers find it difficult to keep track of everything that goes on in the classroom. Older hands seem to spot some things before they actually happen! Monitoring is not separate from the act of teaching; it has to take place at the same time. You may discover that you are so involved in your interactions around the classroom that you fail to spot those children who are making little effort or those struggling with the work. Subsequent intervention can take many forms, including a decision to leave a situation alone. Good teachers are aware of what is happening and let the pupils know they know.

Keynote: To stay alert to what is happening throughout the classroom.

Teaching approach influences the monitoring of learning

Transmission teaching (teacher talking; pupils listening) allows for easier monitoring of behaviour but gives the teacher little information about how much the pupils are learning. Monitoring is more straightforward when the pupils are involved in a set task which leaves the teacher free to circulate, offer advice, ask questions and actively engage with the learning to find out how pupils are progressing. Reactive forms of teaching (when the pupils respond as directed) require that teachers use questions to probe the pupils' understanding or ask for responses as a means of testing their conceptual grasp of issues. Some difficulties may occur through children calling out or getting over-excited. Interactive teaching (initiated by the teacher but where pupils are encouraged to contribute at will) are hardest to control but often give valuable information about pupils' understanding as they attempt to express themselves freely.

Keynote: To monitor appropriately.

Observed behaviour cannot be relied upon as an accurate indicator of pupils' understanding

The quiet child who looks puzzled and does not offer any suggestions, even when invited, may be ignorant of the facts or may need time to think or may be too insecure to say anything (Collins 1996). Such situations are commonplace. Similarly, the child who gives an incorrect answer to a question may not know the answer or may be working to a different agenda. Younger children, in particular, will sometimes affirm loudly that they understand things when, in reality, they are giving a conditioned response which they believe will satisfy their teacher. While you will wish to closely observe children's actions, it is often only by talking to them and allowing them to talk, that you discover their true understanding (see TMS8).

Keynote: To observe children carefully and listen attentively to what they say.

Monitoring and assessment are closely related

Only when pupils are given time to address issues and challenges through practical work, written output, speaking and listening, diagrammatic representations or skills-based processes can you make an accurate assessment of their learning. Even then, with the passage of time, revision and recapping of events and principles will often be needed before learning can be judged to have been satisfactory. Monitoring pupils' progress is a continuous process and provides the information to inform assessment.

Keynote: To monitor as a means of enhancing formative assessment.

Intervention depends on various factors

If the purpose is to allow pupils time to engage with difficult issues that defy easy resolution, or the establishment of cooperative groups to collaborate and debate the issues, intervention is best delayed until children have had opportunity to wrestle with the challenges presented by the lesson. Broad issues about when and where to intervene have to be considered alongside the practicalities of how much support to offer and, in a busy classroom, how much time to spend with individuals, groups and the whole class. It is sometimes desirable to leave children to struggle on with their work rather than intervene too quickly and not give sufficient opportunity for considered thought and grappling with uncertainty. On the other hand, if pupils are left to struggle for too long, they may become restless or disruptive. In the worst scenario, failure to intervene may result in a loss of motivation or loss of class control. You cannot rely on appropriate and successful intervention to ensure an orderly environment if other factors, such as the interest level and relevance of the subject matter, has been neglected (see *FPT*, Chapter 9).

Keynote: To time interventions carefully.

Appropriate intervention is more than responding to signals for help

Some pupils are afraid to ask for help and require sensitive handling; others view teacher support as failure and resist help even when it is offered; yet others rely too heavily on support and benefit from some time alone before being guided. Some pupils develop a dependency upon the teacher which can become obsessive, thereby failing to realise their true potential and stand on their own feet. Whether this is due to fear of failure or has some deeper meaning is not fully understood. One way or another, intervention should not act as a substitute for pupils thinking for themselves. Before you offer your support, consider whether those children asking for assistance could, with prompts and encouragement, gain more by battling through their uncertainties than passively receiving answers from you.

Keynote: To avoid over-dependency.

Intervention does not have to come from the teacher

Pupils cannot learn for others but they can help others learn for themselves. In collaborative settings, the combined knowledge and wisdom of the group can be a positive means of reinforcing learning and helping individuals through their particular struggles. Peer support can suffer from the same constraints as adult intervention, and there are additional problems concerned with the distraction that may be caused to the more able pupil when constantly providing advice to the less able. Parents are sometimes anxious if they believe that their children are being used as a pseudo-teacher. Nevertheless, you will save yourself a lot of time and give pupils opportunity to share their knowledge and skills if you foster a climate of mutual support and cooperation (see TMS1 and TMS11).

Keynote: To encourage a collaborative classroom environment.

Competence check

❑ I am carrying out effective monitoring of work and behaviour patterns
❑ I am giving careful thought to my intervention strategies
❑ I am taking note of the reliance that each child places upon my intervention

TA4 Establish and maintain a purposeful and secure working atmosphere and a good standard of discipline

What you need to take account of…

A purposeful and secure environment takes time to achieve

If you are a student teacher on placement in someone else's classroom, it will take perseverance and courage to establish and maintain a purposeful and secure environment (see *FPT*, Chapter 2). Students enter classrooms in which the class teacher has, it is hoped, already secured the right sort of learning climate. The student teacher's task is, in large measure, to maintain it rather than establish it.

However, if you are meeting groups of children for the first time, you still need to let it be known to pupils that you intend to promote the same rules and expectations that they have been used to with their regular teacher. And don't be lulled into a false sense of security: however delightful the class appears to be initially, the testing time will come. A no-nonsense approach is essential if you are not to spend most of your time on school placement trying to retrieve a situation that you allowed to run out of control by being too passive early on. It is important not to become discouraged if you struggle initially. Establishing a purposeful and secure working atmosphere and good discipline will also depend upon pupils' previous experiences of teachers and their motivation to learn, so some things are beyond your immediate control.

Keynote: To be clear about the sort of learning environment you are trying to achieve.

Pupils take time to adjust to different expectations

As a student teacher, you need to recognise that pupils have become used to their own class teachers' expectations and priorities, so it is wise to adopt the same approach initially. Over time, as you become more familiar with the classroom situation, you will be better able to introduce small changes in the working environment. You may find that in trying to establish your expectations, some pupils become confused or anxious, even protesting that your way is 'not the way it is done here'. Patient, consistent and firm explanation about the way you want things done are necessary. However, if you are unsure whether you may be unintentionally transgressing agreed procedures, it pays not to be too insistent until you have checked it out.

Keynote: To insist without being insensitive to existing norms.

Relationships are built not imposed

Good relationships evolve through shared experiences, clear expectations and rules which are fairly and consistently applied. Above all, pupils do not want to be humiliated, nagged or blamed. Your positive approach, interesting personality and love of learning will help you in your quest for good teacher-pupil relationships. Nonetheless, pupils feel more secure when they are convinced that you know what you are doing and are capable of handling the lesson. They need to be convinced that they have more to gain from cooperation than from lethargy or mischiefmaking. Children will take note of how you relate to individuals (especially the troublesome ones) and your reactions at critical moments. Clear learning objectives, proper resourcing and thinking ahead to predict possible problems, all contribute to a positive working environment.

Keynote: To build productive and positive relationships.

The best type of discipline is self-discipline

All pupils need clear guidance about what constitutes appropriate behaviour, but ultimately they have to decide for themselves that they want to learn more than they want to misbehave. However, some pupils appear incapable of exercising self-discipline without regular insistence from an adult. So don't be afraid to be precise and firm about your expectations. The ideal is to move from a position where pupils do what they are told because you insist, to one where they do so because they choose to. All children need to be reminded from time to time that they are responsible for their own actions and that you expect them to set high standards for themselves.

Keynote: To encourage pupils to be responsible for their own actions.

Well-focused teaching can also be imaginative

As a simple test of what constitutes well-focused teaching, consider whether the average parent, sitting in on your lesson, would understand what you were trying to achieve. In doing so, it is important not to equate being specific with unimaginative teaching methods. On the contrary, the most effective lessons are those in which you use a variety of teaching strategies to achieve the intended aim. If you can capture children's imaginations and appetite for learning by introducing relevant, interesting lessons, you will rarely meet severe discipline problems (see Figure 2).

Keynote: To be a creative teacher.

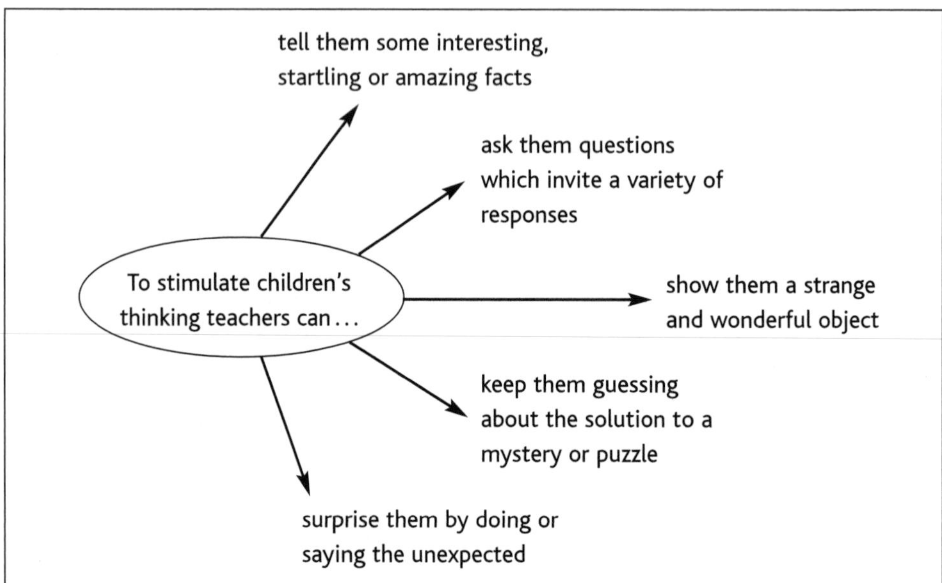

Figure 2 Stimulating pupils' thinking

Competence check

- ❑ Pupils understand what I expect from them
- ❑ Pupils feel that I am in control of the situation
- ❑ The quality of my teaching minimises the likelihood of disruption

TA5 Establish a safe environment which supports learning and in which pupils feel secure and confident

What you need to take account of...

The meaning of a safe environment

A safe environment is one in which pupils feel that the teacher is in control, that they will be able to do their best without having to contend with undue interference from others, and where their efforts will be acknowledged and recognised (see P2 and TMS7). Pupils feel safe when they are protected from bullies, given equal opportunity to use resources and allowed to make genuine mistakes without fear of the consequences. A safe environment is one in which adult–child relationships are courteous, respectful and caring (Noddings 1992). Pupils will not feel safe if they experience humiliation, sarcasm, hectoring or persistent nagging. It is your job to try to provide a learning environment in which lessons are appropriate to the needs of the children, where you explain your expectations clearly, and where you deal with disputes, concerns and upsets in a calm and determined manner. In short, you are both the instigator and the guardian of a safe environment.

Keynote: To allow all children the opportunity to fulfil their potential.

The limitations of your own influence

Although you may feel that you could engender a much healthier atmosphere by adopting a different approach to teaching and learning from the present teacher's, you will not be able to affect the situation markedly in the short time you are in school, and it is more sensible to adopt a strategy of compliance rather than trying to exercise an assertive form of professional autonomy. In short, try to fit in rather than turn the situation upside-down. Accept the class situation as you find it and recognise that you can have a modest but significant impact upon the working environment in small but important ways, rather than being able to transform the situation. When you are the class teacher you will want your students to build on existing structures rather than trying to upset the classroom equilibrium; so be sensitive in your attempts to 'establish' a secure environment.

Keynote: To comply enthusiastically.

Learning and a secure environment should be linked

A secure environment does not necessarily lead to effective learning. Pupils can feel secure without necessarily making a lot of progress. Teaching approaches are sometimes divided into those where teachers are concerned with the affective dimension (that is, developing a close, caring relationship with pupils) and those concerned with the managerial dimension of the role (that is, focusing on attaining measurable outcomes). However, while it is true that different teachers emphasise one or the other, the two dimensions should be seen as closely entwined (like a tapestry) rather than at opposite extremities. The most effective learning takes place when pupils are motivated to work for their own benefit and out of respect for and loyalty to the teacher.

Keynote: To manage pupils' learning skilfully and caringly.

Confidence is a delicate flower

Some children are naturally confident. They seem to ooze self-belief and will have a try at anything. They are first to shoot their hand in the air when you ask for a volunteer and seem to relish challenges. Nothing daunts them. Others are hesitant and prefer the seclusion of anonymity. They have to be encouraged, cajoled and enticed to take a risk. A fear of failure or humiliation handicaps their learning and suppresses their potential (see P5). Most children lie somewhere between the two extremes and may be confident in one situation and hesitant in another. Equally significant is the way in which the same child may be less confident with another teacher. A child who lacks confidence with one teacher may be much more willing with a different teacher who is perceived as more patient and approachable. It is not difficult for teachers to wreck children's confidence through adopting a harsh and unrelenting attitude. It is also true that your understanding and positive manner can help to repair or raise a child's damaged self-esteem. Merry (1998) suggests that children's responses to the likelihood of failing may take many forms, including regression to more infantile and helpless behaviour or venting their frustration on a weaker child. Merry also suggests that children use a variety of strategies to offset the pain of failure (see Table 4). You have to learn to discriminate between those pupils who are too idle to attempt the work and those who are sincerely troubled by concerns over failure. Careful explanations about tasks and appropriately differentiated work will help to offset the worst avoidance problems. If they persist, you may need to spend additional time with the particular children but without making them too heavily dependent upon you.

Keynote: To respect children's sensitivities.

Table 4 Pupils strategies to avoid failing (based on Merry 1998)

- Pupils produce the first answer that comes into their heads
- Pupils only do the easy bits (such as a picture) and neglect the more demanding parts of the work
- Pupils wander around the room while the teacher is occupied with others
- Pupils find reasons to leave the room, especially going to the toilet
- Pupils blame the task, using expressions such as 'This is boring'
- Pupils deliberately avoid listening so as to be genuinely confused
- Pupils do nothing until they are assisted by the teacher
- Pupils work very slowly and make minimal 'safe' progress
- Pupils cheat
- Pupils lose their work, either by destroying it or misplacing it

Children think a lot more than they speak

Some children are slow to express their feelings to adults. Even when children are uncertain, confused or bewildered, they will rarely confide in a teacher unless things become critical, by which time it may be too late to rectify the problem. Students sometimes find out things that are not disclosed to the regular teacher because they are perceived by pupils as being less threatening. This is not invariably true, as sometimes students may themselves be under-confident and fail to establish a satisfactory relationship with the children. Nevertheless, the principle that positive attitudes towards children lead to trust and openness is something that every adult working in school should espouse.

Keynote: To take account of pupils' deeper feelings.

Competence check

- ❑ I have developed a positive working climate in my classroom
- ❑ I have established a sensible balance between the managerial and affective dimensions
- ❑ I am evolving teaching strategies which ensure that all children have opportunity to make optimum progress

TA6 Ensure that pupils acquire and consolidate knowledge, skills and understanding in the subject

What you need to take account of...

Ensuring is a tough requirement

As a teacher, you can make every effort to help pupils acquire knowledge, skills and understanding, but you cannot ensure that what is apparently mastered at one time will be carried forward into new learning. Sometimes, pupils understand something sufficiently well for them to deal with the work in hand, but they do not have an adequate grasp of it to use their learning in new situations. That is, they have failed to create the necessary links between distinct, but related, circumstances. Ensuring that pupils acquire and consolidate knowledge, skills and understanding has to be interpreted in terms of the context and the language competence of the child. Your teaching approach needs to take account of pupils' past experience of learning, the knowledge, understanding and skills that they have gained, and their interest in the subject matter. It is worth remembering that two pupils who superficially appear to have grasped something will still vary in their ability to apply and extend what they have learned.

Keynote: To probe the extent of pupils' understanding.

Knowledge and understanding depend upon perceptions of reality

A nine-year-old might find out that bombs fell on the town during the Second World War, but it is only by speaking to the elderly lady living down the road who survived the onslaught that the knowledge is transformed from a passive piece of information to a dynamic reality in the child's mind. Even then, the child is unable to hear the whistle of shrapnel, the cries of fear and the smell of cordite. Pupils will, depending upon their own experience, imagination and ability to internalise facts, construct an image of bombs falling and causing destruction in the town. The elderly resident will have a more direct form of knowledge due to her lived experience, but may, over time, have created a distorted picture of reality in her mind. Indeed, it is fair to say that if both the child and resident could, in some miraculous way, be transported to the event itself, they would have slightly differing tales to tell of the same situation. Although there are some building bricks of knowledge which necessarily provide the foundation for extended learning, children have to be taught to examine the facts in the light of fresh understanding and experience. The knowledge that you pass on to your pupils will sometimes be absolute and sometimes open to interpretation. Children's understanding relies on the sense that they can make of the evidence with which they are presented and the associated factors that impinge upon the circumstance. As you seek to enhance pupils' knowledge and understanding, it is important to see things as children of that age see them. Ask for their opinions, listen to what they say in reply and take note.

Keynote: To consider the children's perspectives.

Consolidation can be achieved by various means

Consolidation of indisputable facts may best be achieved by repetition; for instance, generations of children have learned their multiplication facts in this way. Consolidation may involve fuller understanding of facts; for instance, the effect of placing a letter 'e' after the final consonant of a word containing 'a' softens the centre vowel (mat becomes mate; rat becomes rate, etc.) but the rule does not operate with every vowel (pot does not transform to pote; get does not become gete, and so on). By looking at the fuller picture, discussing the variations and toying with nonsense words, the original facts become more meaningful and memorable. Consolidation may involve using existing knowledge, skills and understanding in problem-solving or investigative situations; for instance, orientation and mapping skills can be utilised for an environmental project based around the school grounds. All forms of consolidation are enhanced by talking to others about the subject area involved. Many people testify to the fact that they never know that they understand something until they hear themselves explaining it to someone else! (See Figure 3.)

Keynote: To consolidate without confusing.

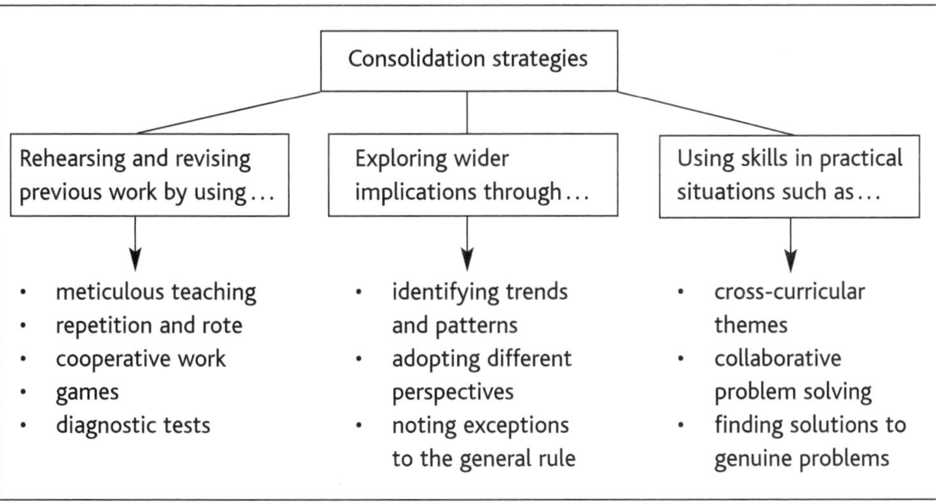

Figure 3 Consolidation strategies

Competence check

❑ I know what knowledge and understanding I want the pupils to acquire

❑ I have taken sufficient account of pupils' age, experience and present understanding

❑ I have incorporated a valid and reliable means of assessing pupils' progress into my planning

CHAPTER 3

Teaching Methods and Strategies (TMS1–12)

Teaching methods and strategies involves the largest number of demands. There are 12 areas in which you must demonstrate your competence:

TMS1	Using teaching methods which result in optimum pupil performance.
TMS2	Matching the approach to the subject and pupils.
TMS3	Structuring the lesson.
TMS4	Clearly presenting content around a set of key ideas.
TMS5	Instructing, demonstrating and explaining.
TMS6	Effective questioning.
TMS7	Using pupils' errors and misconceptions.
TMS8	Listening and responding to pupils.
TMS9	Acquiring the necessary basic skills and study skills to utilise learning resources.
TMS10	Offering opportunities for pupils to consolidate their knowledge.
TMS11	Setting high expectations for all pupils.
TMS12	Developing pupils' wider understanding.

TMS1 Use teaching methods which sustain the momentum of pupils' work and keep all pupils engaged

What you need to take account of...

Teaching methods form part of a total teaching approach

A 'method' suggests a single, specific and definable way of doing things. However, the best teaching methods are sufficiently structured to provide a solid framework for the passage of the lesson and sufficiently flexible to allow for unexpected opportunities. Some inexperienced teachers find that a particular method works in a certain situation and assume that it can be used on every occasion, regardless of context or conditions. It is not uncommon to hear comments such as 'I use stand-and-deliver methods' or 'I rely on group work' or 'I get the children to discover things for themselves'. All of these methods (and many others) are useful but it is unwise to think of any one of them as the answer to a teacher's prayer. The best teachers employ a variety of methods appropriate to the occasion. Table 5 offers some guidelines over making your decisions.

Keynote: To employ a range of teaching methods.

Table 5 Determining the appropriate teaching method

- To give information: use direct transmission
- To examine issues: use explanation followed by discussion
- To teach techniques: use demonstration followed by skills training
- To develop study skills: use explanation followed by activities
- To consolidate previous learning: use activities and tasks
- To extend thinking: use group investigation
- To develop oracy: use group discussion

A method depends on the person using it

Although teaching methods are based to an extent on following familiar procedures and strategies, their effectiveness relies on the quality of your preparation, delivery and competence (see *FPT*, Chapter 6). Some teachers are very effective in a 'stand-and-deliver' mode and can keep the pupils' attention through variety of tone, use of visual aids, stories, poems and lively questioning. Others find that their skills lie more in developing and supporting group activities; yet others will provide interesting worksheets which stimulate and probe pupils' understanding, and so forth. The very best teachers do all of these things. Wherever your talents lie, it is worth exploiting them fully and demonstrating your abilities openly. In areas of teaching where you feel less confident (such as taking the 'up-front' role) it is worth persevering and getting advice about how you might improve your communication skills (Hayes 1998).

Keynote: To utilise teaching strengths fully and address weaknesses resolutely.

Interesting lessons require special effort

Intellectual curiosity is stimulated when pupils' interest has already been engaged and they believe that it is worth making the effort to find out more. You can enhance this interest by projecting a lively curiosity of your own as you introduce the topic and interact with the pupils throughout the lesson. Deadpan expressions and lifeless monotones are certain to create an inert learning climate.

Relevant and interesting lessons have to be presented in attractive ways if children are to be convinced by them. Every child is curious, so exploit their curiosity at every opportunity. Place items in boxes; hide things from sight until the last moment; present the mundane in unusual ways; heighten expectation; celebrate discoveries. Don't forget that things which are commonplace to grown-ups can be a source of delight for young minds. Although it is not advisable to adopt a 'song-and-dance' mentality towards teaching, it is preferable to incline in that direction than being grim and unsmiling.

Keynote: To capture pupils' interest by teaching with flair and imagination.

Pupils' and teachers' motivation vary

In an ideal world, motivation would remain consistently high. In reality, levels are unpredictable and fluctuate from day to day, lesson to lesson, and even during a single session. Motivation is controlled by a complex mix of interest, pupils' previous experiences of the subject, your own enthusiasm and the embedded expectations about teaching and learning that exist in the class and throughout the school (see also TMS11). Some days, teaching is like stirring treacle; on others, it is like hang-gliding. Predicting that some lessons will be a struggle, or explaining why some are successful, is difficult, but it is worth being alert to some of the most powerful influences that may affect lesson planning and delivery (see Table 6).

Keynote: To motivate oneself first of all.

Table 6 Motivation factors

High motivation is likely when:

- teachers and pupils feel happy and relaxed
- the subject matter is interesting and relevant
- teachers have experienced recent success in their teaching
- the classroom climate is safe and secure
- pupils believe that they will be treated fairly
- expectations are clear and achievable
- success is visible and celebrated

Problem solving can be a powerful medium for harnessing the collective wisdom of the group

The lesson purpose is not always about cleanly defined learning intentions; outcomes are frequently far messier than could have been envisaged, particularly when collaborative tasks and dealing with complex dilemmas form the heart of the session. Problem solving is not a substitute for teaching; it is an opportunity for pupils to use the knowledge and understanding which they already possess and exploit them to find answers to questions. There are two broad forms of problem solving: one in which the answer is genuinely unknown (the 'what will happen if' type) and one where the answer is known by the teacher but not by the pupils (the 'find out what the answer is' type). In the first case, a variety of answers may be possible, in which case the problem solving is more correctly called 'investigating'; in the second case, it is likely that there will only be a single or small number of possible solutions (see Table 7). It is important that you ensure that before children are given collaborative tasks of any kind, you have spent time explaining the ground rules and attitudes required for successful completion.

Keynote: To involve pupils in the collaborative effort.

Table 7 Problem solving and investigations

- Problem solving: where there is only one or a strictly limited number of solutions
- Investigations: where there are a variety of possible solutions

Effective teaching involves passion

Passion in teaching can be misconstrued. It can be confused with emotional fervour or even frenzy. In fact, passionate teaching involves the need for clearly defined goals, well-considered beliefs about learning and a determination that every child will benefit from your knowledge, expertise and skills. An important element of passion is caring about what is best for children, in terms of both their academic learning and their social development. Care is not soft or flimsy. It sometimes demands hard choices, firmness, consistency and occasional severity. Children do not thank a teacher for being 'nice' in a feeble way, but rather trustworthy, decent, dependable and informed. Winkley (2002), in his fascinating account of working in a school located in a deprived area of a major city, makes some important points about passion in teaching. He argues that it requires a long-term commitment and an intensity of interest by teachers in the pupils and the subjects they are teaching. It 'acts as an inner fire, burning away' (p. 23). Winkley makes a number of other valuable points, as the following extended quotations make clear (all p. 23):

> A passionate teacher may be quiet and fastidious, just as she may be tough and vigorous; but the pupils know about teachers who are committed to them, and forgive them a lot...

> Such caring is signalled in a large number of small matters. It matters how you speak to me, how you mark my work, how you look at me...
>
> Caring motivates. It not only makes you feel better; it makes you work better. It oils the relationships in the classroom. It enhances the way you value yourself.

Passion in teaching is not about showing pity or allowing children to please themselves. It is about making learning tolerable all of the time, engaging much of the time, and astounding some of the time. It is saying to children through word, action and gesture that because you care, you are going to do everything in your power to motivate and encourage them. Part of the unwritten agreement between you and the children is, however, that they have to respond reasonably and do their best. What more can you ask as a teacher?

Competence check

- ❏ I am willing and able to use a range of teaching methods
- ❏ I have taken account of pupil motivation
- ❏ I am able to enthuse the pupils by my teaching

TMS2 Match the teaching approaches used to the subject matter and the pupils being taught

What you need to take account of...

It is sometimes easier to match the teaching approach to the form of knowledge than to the curriculum subject

A lot depends on what you expect the children to learn. For instance, if you want them to acquire specific knowledge for a limited period of time (i.e. knowledge that only has to be remembered for a short time, such as a specific safety procedure during an educational visit) you will want to explain what is required as quickly and firmly as possible, and monitor the situation until the need to remember has passed. If the knowledge is required over a longer period of time, your approach depends on the type of knowledge involved. For instance, things to be memorised demand a different teaching approach from things that can be found out through reference sources. Whereas the knowledge to be memorised will benefit from repetition, discussion, committing the facts to paper, and so on, information from references requires an understanding of where to look for it, what forms of information to access (books, the Internet etc.) and how to translate the information into useful knowledge. It is relatively easy for children to find out the date and outcome of a famous battle; it is more demanding for them to understand its impact on people's lives and its place in the sequence of events of that time. Although some subjects tend to invite a particular teaching emphasis, the end product of what you want the children to learn and the best way for them to achieve it should dominate your thinking more than the particular curriculum subject (Littledyke and Huxford 1998).

Keynote: To use the teaching approach which facilitates learning.

Practical tasks consolidate learning

Younger children generally benefit from having plenty of opportunity to touch, feel, examine, experiment and discover for themselves. This does not mean that they are incapable of storing information and understanding, but that structured and unstructured play is a valuable way of reinforcing learning and allowing them to extend their thinking. However, involvement in practical activities will not, of itself, ensure enhanced learning. It needs to be part of a total learning programme. There are broadly two ways to approach using practical tasks to assist learning. The first is to introduce topics to the pupils and help them to develop a basic understanding through explanation, examples and demonstration, then set practical tasks as a means of confirming the truth, exploring alternatives or consolidating learning. For instance, to demonstrate that the perimeter of a polygon is the same regardless of whether the measures are taken clockwise or anti-clockwise, then set practical tasks to confirm the validity of the claim. The second approach is to set a problem-solving task at the start of the lesson, giving a strict time limit, then to draw on pupils' findings to establish the principles or key facts. For instance, children may be given the task of finding the speed at which different objects (screwed-up paper, cork, feather, paperclip, conker) fall to the ground (on to a thick newspaper to avoid too much noise!). Subsequently, you can garner all the differing findings and opinions and discuss the laws of gravity and, perhaps, the effect of air pressure on some objects. Children normally enjoy practical tasks but you have to try and ensure that the time is well spent. (See Figure 4.)

Keynote: To set purposeful practical tasks.

Organising for learning requires a knowledge of the individual pupil

You have to make a decision about whether pupils will learn more effectively through individual or collaborative activities, bearing in mind that the children who like to work alone are sometimes the ones who need to experience working in groups. Persuading children to work in groups who prefer to work on their own requires a lot of tact and firm encouragement. On the other hand, children who fear to work alone should not be allowed to rely too heavily on other pupils or yourself. More enterprising lessons should involve a mixture of individual, pair and group activity, even if it has to cover a number of sessions. For instance,

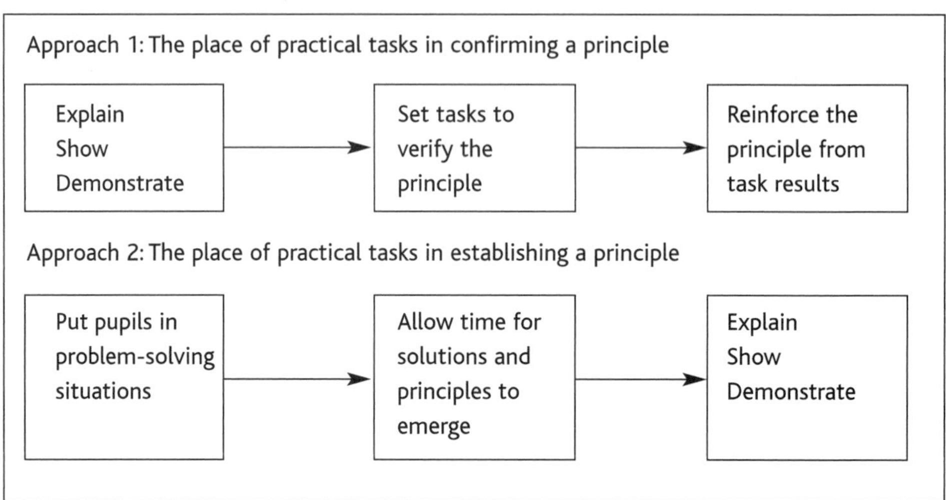

Figure 4 The place of practical tasks in learning

session one might involve considerable teacher input followed by individual work, session two might involve working in pairs, session three might involve collaborative problem-solving tasks. Whatever form of organisation you use, always take account of its manageability and the need to make things clear to pupils concerning the times they are expected to work singly and when they are allowed or encouraged to work with a partner. Forms of organising may look slick on paper but flounder because the needs of particular pupils have not been fully considered. For instance, some children get confused about the distinction between collaborating and cheating. These issues should be discussed and resolved before, and not during the lesson.

Keynote: To take account of individual needs and inclinations.

Different teaching environments require different approaches

Teaching in a classroom-based situation requires different skills from those required in a large-space situation. Organisation has to be extremely thorough and well planned for large-space activities as there are no activity options available in the way there are in the classroom. In the classroom, there are normally paper-and-pencil tasks, small games, finishing-off incomplete work and book resources to use. In the hall or outside it is a matter of children being involved or not involved with all the potential for misbehaviour that being under-occupied brings. At the other extreme, a confined space brings a different set of constraints. In particular, children should move around as little as possible and resources should be distributed and collected by monitors.

Keynote: To take account of room size.

Competence check

- ❑ I am taking account of the subject area when I plan my teaching
- ❑ I incorporate the appropriate mix of direct teaching and practical activity
- ❑ I have made allowances for the particular learning needs of individuals

TMS3 Structure information well, including outlining lesson content and aims, signalling transitions and summarising key points

What you need to take account of...

Information should not be confused with knowledge and understanding

Information has to be interpreted and evaluated before it can be absorbed into a pupil's knowledge system and used actively in learning. For instance, children can learn a song off by heart in a foreign language yet not understand a word! Some children love to accumulate information but have little idea about its use and relevance. If you provide information to pupils, try to explain its significance by using a number of practical examples or demonstrations to consolidate learning. Ensure that they have time to talk about the information and handle it in a variety of ways (through worked examples, practical tasks, etc.) until they see where it fits in with their existing knowledge. Memorising facts is useful; understanding their application is better.

Keynote: To aim for fuller understanding.

Structure alone is insufficient

Content is an important factor in lesson planning but relies upon an active teaching approach to engage the pupils' hearts and minds. It is wise to spend a small amount of time telling pupils about the broad structure of the lesson, together with what you hope they will achieve, what they have to do, how long they have to do it, and where it links with other aspects of learning. Basic details can be written for them on the board or a sheet of paper in advance of the lesson (an example is given in Table 8). Interactive teaching, in which you allow for pupils' questions and reactions, invite opinions, and stimulate thinking, needs to be balanced with periodic summaries of 'so far' and 'therefore'. Your explanations should be well paced and clear, allowing adequate time for pupils to absorb what you are saying and, where relevant, ask for clarification. Regardless of the extent to which lessons are structured, teaching should be active and dynamic, allowing opportunity for pupil involvement and creativity. If the structure is sound, creativity can flourish; if it is unsound, creativity becomes chaos!

Keynote: To develop a purposeful lesson structure.

Table 8 Example of a lesson structure

Topic
Designing and describing products (design and technology)

Organisation
Individually, then in pairs

Task

1. On your own, construct a simple structure from the materials provided that can stand upright without support (10 mins)
2. Write down instructions to make it, using only five steps (10 mins)
3. Give your partner the instructions to follow (10 mins)
4. Watch as your partner makes the structure (5 mins)
5. Discuss how to improve the instructions (5 mins)
6. Write up the new instructions plus a diagram of your model on the clean paper provided

Extension
Incorporate the newly discovered ideas into the 'Inventions' project

Transitions may be planned

Your lesson plan may involve an introduction in which you remind pupils of what has gone before; a short and lively question-and-answer session to stimulate interest; an explanation about the lesson content; a demonstration of correct equipment use; opportunity for questions, comments and points of clarification; collaborative tasks as a means of exploring the relevant concepts and mastering the key skill. The skill with which you move from one lesson element to another will influence the overall lesson success. It is relatively easy to change from (say) time spent on direct-transmission teaching to a question-and-answer session; it is far more difficult to move from direct teaching to the associated practical tasks. It is important to remain fully in control during this transition and give firm, clear and decisive instructions to children about where they should go and what they should do. Avoid the 'scrummage' approach in which you give instructions and then release the children like a bullet from a shotgun as they pepper around the classroom to begin their tasks. Allow only a few children to move at one time, ensuring (of course) that resources are available and adequate for the numbers involved.

Keynote: To keep a firm grip during transitions.

Transitions may be unplanned

However closely defined your lesson preparation may be, there are occasions when your instinct tells you that it is time to move on to another phase. Such moments are signalled when, for instance, the children are getting restless or enthusing about new ideas or suggesting creative possibilities. You have to decide whether to 'go with the flow' and respond to their behaviour, or to maintain the lesson pattern as you originally conceived it. Although pupils should never be allowed to dictate the pattern of a lesson, wise teachers take careful account of their actions and reactions, and adjust accordingly.

Keynote: To take account of the learning climate.

Summaries should be succinct

A summary should be just that! Resist the temptation to launch into new ideas. The end phase of a lesson is always quite demanding, requiring a variety of classroom management skills – summarising the lesson purpose, praising good work and effort, dispensing information about where to put finished and unfinished items, maintaining control, observing the time and ensuring that the room is left tidy – so resist the opportunity to complicate the final few minutes. End on a positive note but do not allow children to leave the room until you are satisfied they have completed what is required. Stay alert until everything is orderly, then dismiss the children as appropriate (see *FPT*, Chapter 9).

Keynote: To pay as much attention to the end phase of a lesson as any other.

Competence check

- ❏ I am clear about whether I am dealing with knowledge or information
- ❏ I have structured my lessons in such a way as to allow for a smooth transition from one stage to the next
- ❏ There is room in my lesson for creativity and innovation

TMS4 Clearly present content around a set of key ideas

What you need to take account of...

Key ideas should link closely with lesson intentions

Content may take the form of factual information, the introduction of ideas, problem-solving situations, experiments, reinforcement activities or a combination of elements. If your lesson is principally concerned with introducing new vocabulary or examining the structure of certain words, the key ideas will be different in kind from one in which the purpose is to master specific practical skills or follow set procedures. A useful way of establishing the key ideas is to try to describe them in a single sentence to someone who knows little about the subject.

Keynote: To link content with lesson purpose.

Accurate and appropriate use of vocabulary is essential if pupils' understanding is to be extended

Pupil puzzlement over terminology is an obstruction to learning. Do not assume that pupils know the meaning of terms, especially subject-specific ones. Spend a little time towards the start of the session introducing or clarifying important words, and throughout the lesson providing necessary explanations. Understanding terminology requires more than being familiar with regular terms; pupils need to be able to handle concepts by using appropriate vocabulary. For instance, in maths pupils need to know the names of common 2-D and 3-D shapes before they can discuss their properties. Words such as 'pitch', 'duration', and 'tempo' are significant when it comes to discussing musical excerpts. It is helpful to encourage the children to incorporate specific terms into their speech and writing when, for instance, they report back or answer questions.

Keynote: To integrate vocabulary with concept development.

Illustrations and examples need to be chosen with care

Younger children tend to accept things literally and find it difficult to interpret metaphors. The challenge is to use appropriate vocabulary that conveys the concept, idea or information for children in a way which is appropriate to their different ages. Examples should be as precise as possible rather than using analogies or inexact comparisons. Primary-age children accept most things at face value; they have neither the maturity nor intellectual sophistication to be able to generalise an example from the particular. This is especially true when attempting to explain deeper truths about moral and spiritual values. For instance, reference to death as someone 'falling asleep' or 'going to heaven' may conjure confusing images for younger children who might fear going to bed at night lest they never wake up or imagining heaven to be full of corpses! Similarly, the expression 'as cunning as a fox' will have a different meaning to town and country children. Even traditional tales about 'wicked step-mothers' take on fresh meaning for children from split homes who now live with a new family.

Keynote: To take account of children's maturity and circumstances.

Terminology should be used consistently and accurately

For instance, the terms 'take away', 'subtract' and 'minus' have a common meaning when used in respect of finding the difference in size between two numbers; but have subtly different meanings when used in specific circumstances. Thus, 'take away' indicates removal of a part from the whole, whereas 'subtract' relies on a comparison between two numbers and 'minus' is used in connection with negative numbers. Similarly, the word 'tone' has a different (though associated) meaning when used in art and music. If terminology is to be used effectively, we must ensure that words are used consistently and understood by the children.

Keynote: To establish a common vocabulary.

Competence check

- ❏ I have thought carefully about the key ideas for the lesson
- ❏ I am using appropriate vocabulary for the age and ability of pupils
- ❏ I have chosen my illustrations and examples with care

TMS5 Offer clear instruction and demonstration, and accurate, well-paced explanation

What you need to take account of...

Effective teaching needs thorough preparation

The most effective direct teaching results from thorough preparation and rehearsal. It is a mistake to imagine that teachers are good 'on their feet' due solely to natural ability. Most effective transmission teaching requires a strong grasp of the relevant facts and their implications, and time spent beforehand considering the best way to deliver the lesson in a meaningful way which allows the children to absorb what is being said. It is one area of teaching that can be usefully rehearsed beforehand, perhaps recorded on an audio cassette or in front of a friend. Listen out for the moments of hesitation which indicate uncertainty and the variety in your tone of voice. Make a deliberate effort to 'write in' pauses (count to five in your head) and anticipate the kinds of questions which children may ask after listening to you. Although a lesson structure may vary from your planned intention, thoroughness of preparation is never wasted (see Figure 5).

Keynote: To prepare thoroughly for direct teaching.

It is essential to clarify the type of direct method you are adopting

Broadly, there are three approaches. The first is when you are transmitting information, using interesting and visual stimuli where appropriate. Second is a

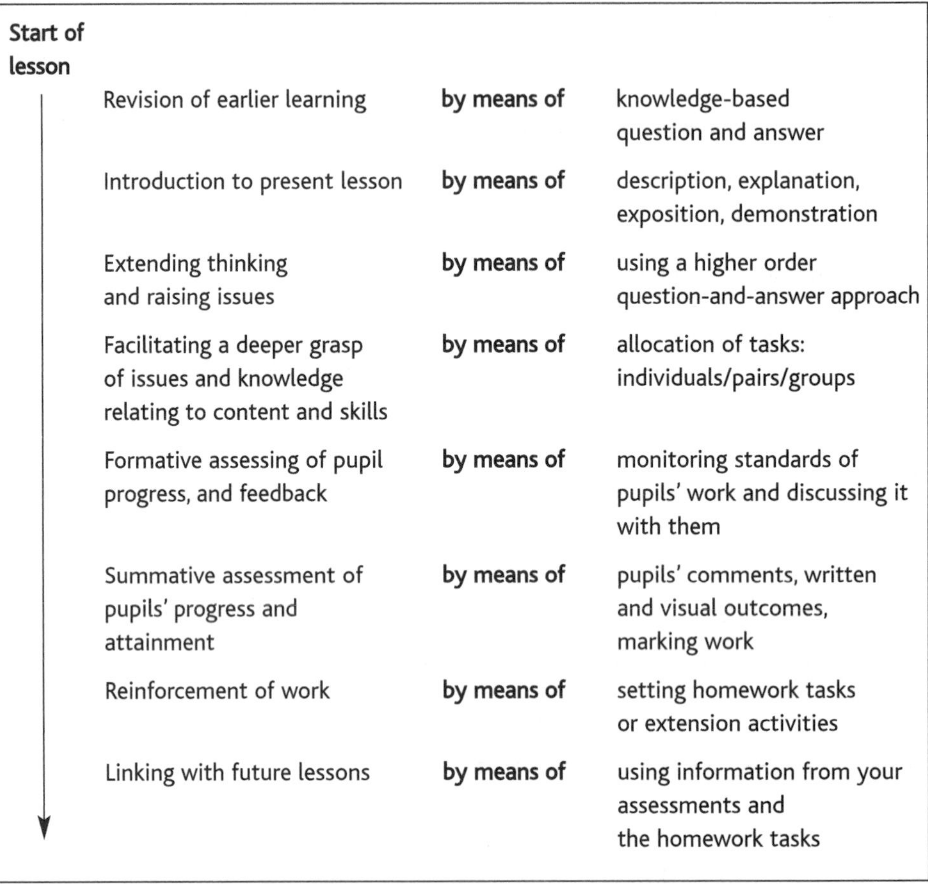

Start of lesson		
Revision of earlier learning	by means of	knowledge-based question and answer
Introduction to present lesson	by means of	description, explanation, exposition, demonstration
Extending thinking and raising issues	by means of	using a higher order question-and-answer approach
Facilitating a deeper grasp of issues and knowledge relating to content and skills	by means of	allocation of tasks: individuals/pairs/groups
Formative assessing of pupil progress, and feedback	by means of	monitoring standards of pupils' work and discussing it with them
Summative assessment of pupils' progress and attainment	by means of	pupils' comments, written and visual outcomes, marking work
Reinforcement of work	by means of	setting homework tasks or extension activities
Linking with future lessons	by means of	using information from your assessments and the homework tasks

Figure 5 The structure of a lesson

reactive approach in which you pose the questions and problematics for pupils to consider and make response towards. Third is an interactive approach in which pupils are able to interrupt, ask their own questions, offer insights and comment without your sanctioning it (see also TMS1). Direct teaching (where you do all the talking) is more straightforward than handling pupil responses. Interactive teaching requires confidence and familiarity with the class.

Keynote: To clarify the form of direct method used.

Effective didactic teaching benefits from a dynamic delivery

Instruction and demonstration demand a direct-teaching approach in which the teacher initiates and controls the pace and content of the lesson. You should make it clear to pupils whether you want to speak uninterrupted, whether you want them to respond in some way (and if so, how), or whether they are allowed to make comments, offer suggestions, raise questions, and so forth. If you are speaking uninterrupted, then the use of an assertive voice, variety of tone and appropriate visual aids are important elements in maintaining pupils' interest and attention. Didactic teaching allows you to project your personality and develop a good rapport. It also invites unwanted comments and restlessness if delivered poorly or unduly extended.

Keynote: To speak with verve and enthusiasm.

Pupils take time to absorb what teachers say

Although you may have spent many hours preparing your lesson, the pupils will be hearing things for the first time. It is therefore essential to explain things carefully and in a spirited manner but without rushing. Small pauses to allow pupils the opportunity to think about what you have said or clarify points will enhance learning. Some children who appear to be uncooperative are trying to make sense for themselves of your confusing instructions. If one line of reasoning or explanation does not appear to be working, it is worth trying a different approach rather than endlessly persevering with the same one. It is easy to get carried away by the sound of your own voice and forget for whom the explanation is intended!

Keynote: To consider the listeners.

Demonstrations require particularly careful preparation

Demonstrations are of two broad types: those in which you are showing something to pupils because it is the best way for them to learn; those in which you are showing basic skills for pupils to use later in their own practical activities. Before commencing a demonstration, it is essential to have resources near at hand, to stand where all pupils can see and hear, and to have key words and ideas written beforehand on the board or cards (to reduce the amount of time spent with your back to the class writing things down). Before you show pupils how to do something, it is important to be sure that they have already mastered elementary ideas, skills and vocabulary associated with the topic.

Keynote: To know what is being demonstrated and the practicalities of carrying it out.

Competence check

- ❏ I have thought through exactly what I am going to say and how I am going to say it
- ❏ I am speaking at an appropriate pace with adequate pauses
- ❏ I am injecting some vitality into my teaching

TMS6 Provide effective questioning which matches the pace and direction of the lesson and encourages all pupils to participate

What you need to take account of...

Questions form an important part of teaching

Your lesson preparation should place questions you intend to ask under three basic forms: those for which there is only one answer; those for which there are a limited number of correct answers; those for which there are a variety of possible answers depending on individual opinions. Good questions stimulate thought, create interest, encourage pupils to think, explore ideas and consider alternatives. As questioning involves an interactive form of teaching, make certain that you have good class control and some basic rules of courtesy and procedure. If you ask a question to which there is no definite answer or uncertainty, it is better to say so at the start rather than trying to give the impression that everything is clear-cut; however, make certain that you find out the answer as soon as possible or guide the children to do so on your behalf. You will benefit from showing as much enthusiasm for finding out as you expect from your pupils.

Keynote: To use questions constructively.

Questions can seem threatening to pupils

Some children stick their hand in the air at every opportunity. Others become nervous about answering questions publicly and it may be a long time before they feel confident enough. It is, of course, essential to treat all answers seriously, even if they are incorrect, as an abrupt reaction to children's tentative responses may damage their confidence for a long time. A useful way of gaining pupils' trust, and allowing timid children to absorb some reflected glory from their confident peers, is to wait until someone provides the correct answer, then ask the rest of the class who else knew the answer, commending them accordingly as the hands are raised. Alternatively, if there is a single answer to the question, give two possible endings (one correct, one incorrect) and ask those who think that the first answer is correct to wink at their partner; then those who think that the second is correct to wink with both eyes. After you reveal the right answer, ask those who guessed correctly to raise their hands. If the question invites a variety of answers, write all of them on the board as they are suggested by the children, number them, and take a vote about which answer is most convincing. Allow the children to vote for (say) three of the answers and draw up the first, second and third choices overall. Although you cannot utilise this complex approach too often, it will help children to appreciate that questions are meant to assist them in knowing and understanding rather than catch them out. By treating all answers seriously (other than on those occasions when children are being deliberately silly, when it is best to ignore them) you should signal to pupils that you value their willingness to try. A cold, dismissive or abrasive response will indicate to more timid pupils that it is better to keep quiet than to incur your wrath.

Keynote: To take account of pupils' concerns in framing questions.

Teachers tend to ask questions for assessment purposes

It is rare for teachers to ask questions because they genuinely do not know the answers and believe that the pupils can provide them! The majority of questions are used as an assessment tool whereby the teacher wants to see how well pupils respond to them based on the work in hand. Assessment questions to which there is a single answer should be used as a means of checking that pupils understand and reminding others about the facts. You should take special note of pupils' answers which indicate that further work is necessary in the area covered by the questions. Your future lesson planning should be modified on this basis.

Keynote: To use assessment questions formatively.

Questions can be used at a variety of levels

It is best to use straightforward questions initially, followed by more involved and challenging ones which can be introduced as pupils are reminded of fundamental points and grasp basic concepts. For instance, you may ask a question about the name of a mountain range (Snowdonia, say) and about the name of a range of hills (Brecon Hills, say) which probe the distinguishing features of a 'mountain' and 'hill'. Depending on the age of the children, further questions may invite answers about characteristics of hills and mountain ranges, their composition and use (recreation, water-power supplies, wildlife, and so on). With careful prompting, children quickly provide stories and instances from their holiday experiences, and information from programmes they have seen and books that they have read. At the end of this interactive time, it is important to return to the fundamental questions which underpin your lesson objectives. For example, it is interesting to know that Elizabeth saw a baby lamb on her weekend walk, but does little to extend the class's understanding of weathering and erosion if this was the key element of the lesson!

Keynote: To layer questions conceptually.

Pupils should develop a questioning attitude

Teachers have a responsibility to create a questioning environment by valuing pupils' questions. Pupils will ask questions when they are interested to know the answers. They will become interested when you engage their hearts and minds and provide lessons which stimulate and enrich their intellects. You will know that you are succeeding in creating such an atmosphere when children become desperate to find out and are willing to persevere and ask questions publicly to do so.

Keynote: To stimulate a desire in pupils to discover more.

Some questions are unanswerable

Learning to live with uncertainty is something that primary-age pupils find very difficult. Issues tend to be clearly defined in their minds and it may take a long time for them to appreciate that dilemmas and paradoxes are as much a part of life as clear-cut solutions. In ethical and moral areas, in particular, it is worth spending a little time in explaining alternatives to children or allowing them to offer opinions before attempting to provide satisfactory answers. Children have to learn to accept that some questions do not have a straightforward answer and others do not appear to have any.

Keynote: To embrace uncertainty.

Questions should not be used as a precursor to a telling-off

If pupils associate questions with subsequent scoldings, their attitude to questioning may be damaged. Such instances include: asking a question and telling off the child for not knowing the answer; asking a question with a threatening tone and, when the child admits responsibility, rewarding honesty with nagging; asking a question and sighing or making a sarcastic comment at the child's expense. In cases of indiscipline, it is tempting to use such a harsh tone when enquiring about the circumstances such that only the most courageous children would dare own up. Consequently, children are tempted to lie and spend the next few minutes defending their innocence against a chorus of accusations from fellow pupils. By asking the question in a moderate, non-threatening but serious tone, it is more likely to receive an honest reply. Even if the child admits to something naughty, approve their honesty without detracting from the seriousness of the behaviour by prefacing what you say with words to the effect: 'Thank you for telling me the truth, but I think that you know that what you did was wrong…'.

Keynote: To use questions positively.

Competence check

- ❏ I am clear about my reasons for using questions
- ❏ I am using a variety of open and closed questions
- ❏ I am encouraging children to adopt a questioning approach

TMS7 Take careful note of pupils' errors and misconceptions, and help to remedy them

What you need to take account of...

Mistakes are a natural part of learning

The saying that 'the person who has never made a mistake has never made anything' is a useful maxim for classroom learning. If pupils are made to feel that there is no room for error in their work, they are likely to become defensive or refuse to attempt things for fear of getting them wrong (see TA5). It is important to make the distinction between mistakes which occur as a result of negligence and those which come from misunderstanding or ignorance. Children who earnestly strive to do their best should be praised and encouraged; those who are apathetic or slothful are, of course, less entitled to sympathy.

Keynote: To put mistakes into perspective.

Pupils like to get things right

It is not always easy to persuade children that mistakes are inevitable and can be used positively. Younger children, in particular, love to see a page of ticks, smiley faces and 'well done' comments. You may need to work hard to convince pupils that although it is preferable to get things correct, it is better to try to get things wrong than not to try at all. A lot depends upon the type of work being undertaken. For instance, if children are attempting to find the answers to a number of computation problems, their ability to find the correct answer is axiomatic to the lesson. In such situations children are pleased to do well and deserve congratulation; however, a raw score may not tell the whole story, for some children may do less well because they have been prepared to attempt more innovative methods to arrive at the answer which will, in the long term, provide the basis for a deeper understanding of the process. It is easy to emphasise the number of correct answers to such an extent that those children searching for alternative solutions may revert to the tried and tested ways to avoid being stigmatised as failures. In your enthusiasm to see pupils gain increasingly higher marks, do not overlook the courageous minority.

Keynote: To put correct and incorrect answers into perspective.

It takes time to get to the root of mistakes

It is tempting to correct mistakes without finding out why the error was made. Asking the child to explain his or her thinking is a powerful means of understanding pupils' thought processes and adjusting your teaching on future occasions. If a child reveals a flawed understanding, a brief clarification will often suffice. There are occasions, however, when a longer explanation will need to form part of a future lesson. The problem with large classes and a busy schedule is that teachers often do not have the time or opportunity to ask questions which probe pupils' understanding; consequently, teaching becomes a mechanical process of setting tasks, marking the results and assessing the children's progress solely on that basis. If you develop the habit of asking pupils about why they have proceeded in particular ways, you will gain unexpected insights into their thinking.

Keynote: To get to the root of pupils' errors.

Determine the error's significance

Making a decision about what is significant requires a great deal of professional judgement. A lot depends on the lesson's intentions. For example, a spelling mistake is significant if the lesson is largely about correct English but relatively insignificant during a brainstorming session when ideas are being thrown down on paper. Similarly, misreading a portion of text may be vitally important when mastering vital health and safety information but relatively unimportant when reading a humorous tale. You may decide to overlook mistakes if pointing them out would disrupt the proceedings unnecessarily, as you can always return to the mistake at a later stage if necessary. On the other hand, to allow an error to remain unchallenged may, in some cases, allow wrong ideas to become embedded in pupils' minds. It can be helpful to preface an intervention with words to the effect: 'Well done to get so much correct. May I point out one thing that you have got confused about...' or similar.

Keynote: To differentiate between serious and trivial errors.

Remedies take differing amounts of time

A casual error (e.g. incorrect punctuation or multiplication) can be corrected quite easily. Indeed, many children will often self-correct if you ask them to look again at their work. More substantial errors may reveal a wholly wrong or confused understanding about the subject. In this case, it will take time to revise previous concepts, re-teach forgotten skills or educate into ways of thinking. The five-year-old who holds a pencil incorrectly can be shown the proper way until, with gentle reminders and appropriate demonstrations, the problem soon passes. By contrast, the ten-year-old who cannot tell the time is clearly going to need a lot of help. Children who do not grasp fundamental skills and concepts will rarely catch up quickly, despite your endeavours on their behalf, though it is possible that your carefully worded explanation and response to a pupil's elementary questions can lead to a sudden surge in understanding. Most of teaching involves continuous effort and application, including a willingness to spend time on a one-to-one basis with the pupil and involve parents where appropriate.

Keynote: To take account of time factors in remedying mistakes and misunderstandings.

If one child has misunderstood, it is certain that others will have, too

When a pupil's error comes to light, other children will not necessarily admit that they share the uncertainty or misconception. More often, the other children who have made similar errors will attempt hurriedly to conceal their mistakes by rubbing out what they have written or changing their response. This defensive reaction results in superficial and contrived improvement which fails to tackle the underlying problems. Pupils' willingness to admit their mistakes is one indicator of the strength of the teacher-pupil relationship. Take note of any error which you notice in several pieces of work and either deal with it by stopping the whole class and talking about the matter there and then, or incorporating it into the next suitable teaching session.

Keynote: To be alert to pervasive problems.

Significant errors should be recorded in writing

It is important to make a record of significant and (especially) widespread errors, for three main reasons: so that you can adjust future lesson plans accordingly; to give yourself opportunity to reflect upon their significance when you evaluate your lessons; to consider what they tell you about ways in which you might improve your teaching. They also assist you when it comes to formal assessment of pupils' work for reporting to parents. It is unwise to assume that you will necessarily remember things. Find a way of making a rapid record in advance of writing it down more carefully after school, such as carrying a small notebook, having a piece of paper on the back of the stock cupboard door or using a dictaphone.

Keynote: To use the assessment of errors as a basis for recording and reporting to parents.

Competence check

- ❑ I have a positive attitude towards pupils' mistakes
- ❑ I have taken time to analyse the underlying cause of the mistakes
- ❑ I have a firm idea about the number of pupils who struggle with similar difficulties

TMS8 Listen carefully to pupils and respond constructively to take their learning forward

What you need to take account of...

A speaking and listening classroom has to be developed

Some teachers discourage children from speaking other than when given permission. Other teachers believe that free and natural speech is essential for effective learning. You have to decide what you are prepared to allow. If you want pupils to have opportunity to speak, you will need to structure your lesson in such a way that it facilitates their contributions within an orderly framework. Finding a balance between encouraging pupils' verbal expression and maintaining an orderly climate is not easy; however, insistence upon basic rules such as not calling out, taking turns and waiting until others have finished speaking provide a helpful structure within which speaking and listening can be enhanced. Student teachers must be careful to take note of what the class teacher presently allows and making gradual adjustments to the interactive pattern after consultation.

Keynote: To encourage constructive talk.

Teachers need to be sensitive to learning opportunities

Pupils can learn facts, understand concepts or gain skills. They can also learn about tolerance, uncertainty, dilemmas and relationships. Learning may take the form of 'learning how to learn' or where to access information or when to speak and when to remain silent. Learning encompasses a range of social, practical and cerebral skills. The nature of your reactions and responses act as a marker for pupils' perceptions about what needs to be known and understood, and what kind of personal interactions are acceptable in the classroom. You have the responsibility of determining whether pupil responses are due to genuine confusion, conceptual difficulty, misunderstanding, unwillingness to engage with work, or a combination of several factors.

Keynote: To see learning opportunities everywhere.

Teachers sometimes talk too much

If you talk too much, pupils will listen to your words but not really hear what you are saying. They may nod their heads and sit bright-eyed looking in your direction, but information overload will deaden rather than kindle their enthusiasm for learning. Some inexperienced teachers find it difficult to sustain a period of transmission teaching; others say too much. Whatever is said, however, you must use appropriate vocabulary and pitch your words at a conceptual level suitable to the age and ability of the children. Remember, too, that the tone of your voice is just as important as the words themselves. For instance, a mysterious tone invites curiosity; a speculative tone suggests that more thinking is needed.

Keynote: To speak concisely.

Teachers sometimes fail to grasp what pupils say

Classrooms are busy places and it is tempting to half-listen to what pupils say (Brown and Wragg 1993) rather than understand what they are trying to tell you. Many teachers find that in order to hurry things along they interrupt children and put words in their mouths rather than allowing them to express things in their own way. Children who are struggling to frame their words will need special patience. Stern (1995) suggests that it is damaging to teacher-pupil relationships if teachers go through the motions of listening without really doing so. Real listening involves teachers trying to understand pupils when what they say makes little sense, accepting the pupil's viewpoint even when they disagree and giving their full attention to what the pupil is saying. Pupils appreciate teachers who give them support but trust them to deal ultimately with the issues, give space for mistakes to be made and offer them enough time to think things through thoroughly and make their own decisions.

Keynote: To be an active listener.

Constructive responses lead to improved understanding and motivation

Constructive responses involve learning to hear what pupils are saying 'beyond the words themselves' and offering encouragement for them to persevere with what they are trying to express through positive body language (such as nods and smiles) and comments (such as 'yes' and 'I understand what you're trying to say'). Children need to know that they are being taken seriously, so the more that you can use their ideas as a basis for developing discussion or shaping the work, the more they will feel that it is worth taking the risk of offering an opinion. Even unusual verbal contributions can provide a stimulus for further debate and clarification of the position. It is sometimes worth checking that you have understood what a child has said by responding with, 'Are you saying that . . .' and re-phrasing what they have said. It is, of course, possible to respond unconstructively, with a resulting deterioration in motivation. Pupils do not appreciate being hectored and lectured on the altar of teachers' frustrations.

Keynote: To value pupils' contributions.

Competence check

- ❑ I am encouraging constructive classroom talk
- ❑ I am really listening to what the children are saying
- ❑ I am setting a good example with my own use of language and talk

TMS9 Exploit opportunities to improve pupils' basic skills

What you need to take account of...

Basic skills are age and ability related

Basic skills evolve and develop as pupils become more sophisticated in their understanding and experienced in their knowledge application. However, most foundation skills need to be revised and reinforced regularly to remind pupils of their significance and ensure that they are firmly embedded in their thinking. Although some younger children may be well advanced academically, they are normally less mature than older children of similar ability. In grouping for learning, especially in classes with more than one year group, there is a need to consider both academic and maturity elements.

Keynote: To take account of competence and maturity.

Some study skills are essential

Study skills rely heavily upon pupils' ability to read, discover facts, classify information, and record appropriately. The ability to skim and scan is particularly important and requires regular, structured lessons to ensure that pupils have an increasingly thorough grasp of it. The Literacy Hour is often based around sections of a relevant text which form the heart of a whole-class lesson lasting between 45 minutes and one hour. The acronym used to describe the structure of the lesson is DARTS, standing for Directed Activities Relating to Texts (see Figure 6). Similarly, unless pupils are capable of manipulating number bonds, they will struggle with many areas of mathematics, and the Numeracy Hour is intended to support this key objective. However, as with all skills, it is essential to offer pupils opportunities to use study skills in a variety of contexts, through thematic and project work.

Keynote: To build strong foundations.

Individual study skills involve confidence and independence

The availability of information is only one element of gaining knowledge. Once access to the information has been secured, pupils have to be trained and directed about ways of recording and using their newfound knowledge. Although it may not be prudent or realistic to write everything down or print everything out, the search

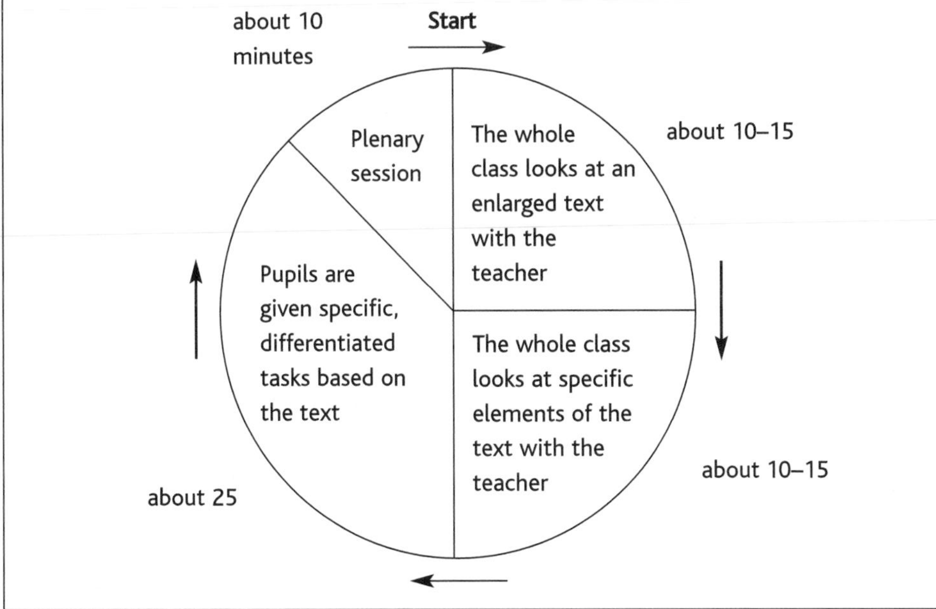

Figure 6 Directed Activities Relating to Texts (DARTS)

for knowledge is most effective when it influences decisions and ideas. Some children take time to gain confidence in their own judgement and require careful guidance from an adult or another child before they risk committing anything to paper. Others assume that they must use every scrap of information which is slightly relevant to the topic. You have the difficult task of ensuring that each child has sufficient confidence and discrimination to know where to look for information and process what is found. Confidence will grow as you systematically teach study skills; independence comes as you give pupils opportunity to develop their skills through access to information sources (see Table 9).

Keynote: To cultivate self-responsibility for learning.

Table 9 Developing independence in learning

Children need to know and understand the following:

- where to look for information and advice
- how much adult support is available
- how long to persevere before seeking help
- what to do with information once it has been found
- how much to record
- how much to share subsequently with others

Information technology is a significant contributor to learning

The growth of information and communication technology (ICT) in recent years has led to the establishment of computer-generated systems in all schools. Children often have machines at home and become adept at handling technology. Using ICT tools is relevant to support learning in all primary school subjects. Pupils have to be taught to

- use a variety of sources
- select information appropriately
- be discriminating in the use of information
- develop and amend ideas through the use of tools
- exchange information electronically
- evaluate their progress and quality of work.

Teachers need to be vigilant to ensure that the enjoyment of using ICT is not at the expense of its principal function; namely, to act as a knowledge source. Pupils will require as much guidance over selection as those using more traditional written information. Although computers have brought benefits in terms of the way they allow access to information, including their appeal to children who struggle with conventional forms of recording ideas and their graphic capability, it is important to be alert to a number of potential disadvantages: the over-use of the computers by a small number of children at the expense of others; the possibility of time-wasting with programs of a relatively low conceptual level; the loss of traditional writing and drawing skills. Although many primary schools are becoming more technologically sophisticated, there are important classroom management issues to consider, including equal opportunity, monitoring the amount of time pupils spend using equipment, safety factors (such as the danger of eye strain) and the location of resources. If equipment is located in special bays or rooms outside the main classroom area, lesson organisation needs to take special account of supervision factors. Information technology, like every other contributor to learning, must be used effectively. You should no more let children loose with computers without adequate training and supervision than you should with books, science equipment or hockey sticks!

Keynote: To make effective use of IT equipment.

There will be wide variance in pupils'experience of ICT

It is important to be aware that some pupils may have a greater understanding and experience of information and communication technology than their teachers. Children spend many hours on their home-computer system, especially playing games, sometimes aided and abetted by a parent or an older sibling. By contrast, school technology can seem quite dull and constraining. Other pupils will not have access to computers at home, so their experiences at school become even more significant. Computer-literate children may try to dominate the use of machines in school; on the other hand, it is useful to be able to draw on their expertise whenever possible. Use of information technology not only has to be differentiated in terms of the programs used but must also take into account the experience, confidence and expertise of individual pupils.

Keynote: To assess pupils' ability and aptitude with ICT.

Resources must be available and accessible

Careful classroom organisation and procedures for safeguarding teaching aids are essential if learning is to be enhanced. Care needs to be taken over the siting of equipment, safety factors and maintenance. Faulty equipment is a source of frustration and can consume your time when you need to concentrate on other aspects of a lesson. Even basic resources need to be properly managed: a tin full of blunt pencil crayons is little use to anyone! If a large amount of equipment is being used (such as different types of balances for work in maths) you have to make the decision about whether to place the balances on tables in advance of the children coming in to the classroom or distributing them after you have introduced the lesson. In the majority of cases, it is better to have items out of reach until they are needed. Attention to practical detail pays dividends in facilitating a smooth-running lesson.

Keynote: To think carefully about resource implications.

Resources should not dictate the pattern of a lesson

Although sets of text books and other information sources are extremely useful to busy teachers, it is unwise to rely wholly on them to guide your lesson preparation and activities. It is easy to fall into the habit of basing your teaching around the resources rather than using them to enhance and improve pupils' learning. For instance, if standard texts are going to provide helpful information or examples for practice or stimulating ideas, then you should not hesitate to use them. When you are stuck for a fresh approach or simply run out of time to produce lesson plans, a published version can be a life-saver, but it is easy to become over-reliant on it at the expense of using your own initiative.

Keynote: To view resources as servants.

Text books have a variety of uses

A text book may or may not be useful in your teaching and depends principally upon the lesson purpose. Some books are inappropriate or confusing; the majority offer some help but are rarely perfectly aligned to what you are trying to achieve, as the author has not, of course, ever had to teach your class. Most books have something useful in them which can be extracted and developed. They can provide examples to thoroughly master something that has already been encountered or questions to extend understanding. Sets of identical texts can be used in collaborative groupings as a means of providing direction, or individually to encourage study skills. Identical texts are particularly useful for group reading procedures in which children all contribute by reading aloud, supported in many cases by the presence of an adult (such as a teaching assistant). Select with care and check the contents carefully before use. Take care not to breach copyright through illegal photocopying; all books contain clear information about what you are allowed to do.

Keynote: To use discretion when selecting texts.

Reference books should be used effectively

A reference book may contain some useful information relevant to the subject area in hand; however, it is rare for one book to contain everything that is needed. You have to make a decision about the extent to which you direct pupils' use of the books.You can allow them to skim and scan, use the index and make arbitrary selections of the information that seems useful; this approach tends to lead to large-scale copying from books and the inclusion of inappropriate sections, but encourages greater pupil autonomy. Alternatively, you can pre-select the books and provide more specific directions for use; this approach focuses the learning, but tends to limit pupils' initiative. Try to avoid the situation in which pupils are endlessly scanning books for a snippet of information for long periods of time when, with some specific guidance from you, they could have found the information easily. If you are helping children to develop study skills, there is some merit in leaving pupils to struggle for a time so that they can understand the need to have strategies for cutting through the large amounts of material. Nevertheless, if you want children to use resources skilfully, you will have to teach them how to be selective, use an index, scan text, and extract appropriate information.

Keynote: To ensure that pupils can access reference material successfully.

Competence check

- ❑ I have ensured that pupils have acquired the necessary study skills to support their learning
- ❑ I am providing the right kind of support for pupils in their use of library resources and ICT
- ❑ I am being discriminating in my use of printed texts and IT

TMS10 Provide opportunities for pupils to consolidate their knowledge, both in the classroom and through setting well-focused homework

What you need to take account of...

Use pupils' existing knowledge

Pupils must have some understanding or level of skill which can act as a basis for further development. Ascertaining the extent of children's existing knowledge can be done through talking to them, asking them to complete an elicitation exercise, carrying out a brainstorming session with groups or the class, examining records of previous work. Many teachers try to 'map' children's existing knowledge by using a spider diagram, beginning with a key term and drawing lines from this term to other words and ideas suggested by the children, until a web of interlocking links has been produced. Alternatively, children can be divided into groups to produce their own diagrams (including pictures as appropriate), allowing the teacher to circulate, listen in to the discussions and make note of significant comments. Encouraging pupils to map their ideas in this way on a regular basis (say, once every half term) can be used as a way of monitoring their understanding of concepts.

Keynote: To find out how much children already know.

Pupils do not have an identical knowledge base

Despite efforts to ensure that all pupils reach or exceed national norms in core subjects, differences in their ability, aptitude and motivation mean that you will always need to spend time reviewing and revising previous learning as a way of ensuring that some basic knowledge can be assumed for the vast majority of the class. By the time children reach the end of their reception class, a considerable variation in their ability and propensity for learning will already be evident. When they leave primary school, it is likely that some children will be struggling to reach Level 2 or 3 in core subject assessments whereas able ones will be at Level 5 or 6. The majority will, of course, fall between these extremes. These variations mean that however much you differentiate the work, some children will always be at the lower or higher end of the spectrum, even if tasks and activities are tailored for them. It is important to recognise that even if all the children had an individual curriculum, ideally suited to their learning needs, there would still be areas to revise, reinforce and develop. In reality, there will always be some things that children forget, misunderstand and fail to grasp adequately, requiring diligence on your part to detect weaknesses and build on strengths.

Keynote: To take nothing for granted.

Consolidation should follow direct teaching

Some inexperienced or hard-pressed teachers imagine that the use of a well-considered worksheet with lots of problems on it (in mathematics, say) provides the ideal way for children to consolidate their understanding of key concepts. However, unless they are already clear about the principles and ideas associated with the subject matter in hand, the use of a worksheet (or other consolidation techniques) will only result in a lot of mystified and frustrated children asking you the same question repeatedly until you are forced to stop the class and explain things to everyone; which is what you ought to have done in the first place. Learning can, and does, take place through exploratory, investigative and play methods, but you need to be clear in your mind about when the children are working towards a learning outcome and when you are helping them to consolidate previous learning. Unless you are specific about the learning intentions for the class, and monitor the pupils' progress carefully, you will not be in a position to know how much consolidation is necessary and when you can press on to the next stage of the learning process. If you underestimate the pupils' grasp of the subject area, you may unwittingly spend too much time consolidating. If you overestimate, you may move on to the next stage before it is appropriate to do so. Regular assessment of pupils' understanding and abilities therefore play a crucial role in determining the right time.

Keynote: To consolidate existing knowledge and understanding.

Some pupils require longer to consolidate than others

It would be wonderful if every pupil progressed at an identical rate. Lesson preparation would be simple; assessments could be carried out in the firm assurance that results would be consistent across the class; consolidation exercises would equally enhance every pupil's grasp of the work, and all the beautifully presented documentation about stages of learning and idealised models of pupil progress would make perfect sense. Unfortunately, learning is not that simple and some children struggle with concepts or mastery while others proceed without a hitch; on other occasions, the children who found certain work easy now find that it is their turn to struggle while others sail through. Such is the nature of learning. The reality of the learning process ensures that smooth and uninterrupted progress exists only in the minds of those who do not have to teach your class! Some children require a lot of support and extra practice; others do not. Some children have to persevere in a way which is unnecessary for the majority. Consolidation is therefore not identical for every child: it may take the form of revising fundamental principles; it may be to refresh children's memory and re-awaken interest; it may act as a spur to further learning. In many cases, consolidation fulfils all these requirements.

Keynote: To allow adequate time for consolidation.

Worksheets should be used constructively

Worksheets (activity sheets) are a useful means of ensuring that a sizeable group of children are engaged on a defined task, thus allowing you to give closer attention to specific children. However, overuse of sheets can lead to tedium and a stale atmosphere as pupils churn through one after another without reflecting on what they are doing or talking about their understanding of the subject area. Although worksheets may serve a useful function in helping to reinforce learning, they have the disadvantage of creating endless amounts of marking and are too often only half-completed or left to gather dust in the bottom of trays. By contrast, the old adage that 'we don't know what we think until we have heard ourselves express it' is a valuable principle governing consolidation. This can be achieved through class or group discussion, written accounts and visual representations. Problem-solving and investigative activities allow pupils to sharpen their newfound understanding and skills on the cutting stone of discovering creative solutions (see also TA6).

Keynote: To use worksheets imaginatively.

Setting and marking homework has time implications

This is true for both pupils and teachers. You have to spend time preparing and explaining the homework; pupils have to complete it; you have to assess or monitor what is done; pupils have to respond to your comments, and so forth. Time factors need to be incorporated into your weekly planning overview and allowance made for the additional demands that will fall on you in managing the process. Even if your school runs a homework club (or similar), time constraints in respect of monitoring and assessing still have to be considered. With the time demands generated through a homework system, it is essential to keep the process transparent and organisationally simple. Elaborate systems cannot be sustained for long as the realities of the working world impinge upon the best-laid plans. All sorts of factors affect the process, such as child absence, timetable alterations, lost books and so forth. It is also important to remember that children work at different rates at home in much the same way as they do in school, so homework tasks must take account of these variations. It is unreasonable to set the same task for the whole class which some children can do in ten minutes and others are unable to complete despite many hours of trying. The best homework tasks are those which follow on from the day's lessons; however, it is not always possible or desirable to be rigidly systematic. A satisfactory solution is to balance a regular homework task (such as reading several pages of a set text) with innovative tasks which cover a longer period of time (such as a half term) in which pupils use a variety of study skills to discover more facts about a topic or completion of a booklet containing interesting, open-ended tasks (see also P3).

Keynote: To be realistic about what can be achieved through homework.

There is a difference between managing and assessing homework tasks

Reading several pages of a text each night is usually managed through a 'reading record' in which parents write down the progress their children have made (such as pages read, words encountered, problems arising) and teachers take account of the comments and occasionally add their own. The assessing of homework involves the more demanding task of testing, marking or in some way evaluating the progress that pupils have made as a result of doing it. For instance, if every child has completed a page of English comprehension, you have to spend time going through the passage, reviewing progress and providing feedback. The work has to be collected in and marked, returned to pupils and issues arising from the task subsequently picked up in class lessons. There is little point in setting a formal homework and failing to assess the resulting product. A lot of exciting homework ideas are impractical due to the heavy assessment demands they generate.

Keynote: To take account of assessment factors when setting homework tasks.

Competence check

❏ I understand what children already know
❏ I am distinguishing between teaching and consolidating
❏ Homework is enhancing children's understanding of what they already know

TMS11 Set high expectations for all pupils notwithstanding individual differences

What you need to take account of...

Effective learning opportunities must be provided for all pupils

The National Curriculum 2000 (DfEE/QCA 1999) requires that planning a school curriculum must provide the starting point for meeting the needs of individual children and groups of pupils. That is, that 'teachers should aim to give every pupil the opportunity to experience success in learning and to achieve as high a standard as possible' (p. 30). Furthermore, teachers should set 'high expectations for boys and girls, pupils with special educational needs, pupils with disabilities, pupils from all social and cultural backgrounds, pupils of different ethnic groups including travellers, refugees and asylum seekers, and those from diverse linguistic backgrounds' (p. 31). Three principles for developing a more *inclusive* curriculum underpin these challenging requirements:

(a) Setting suitable learning challenges.
(b) Responding to pupils' diverse learning needs.
(c) Overcoming potential barriers to learning and assessment for individuals and groups of pupils.

In attempting to ensure that every pupil experiences success in learning and feels confident about his or her ability, account should be taken of unusual circumstances (e.g. extended absence) by *differentiating* tasks and activities to accommodate children with exceptional problems/abilities. For example, a child who has been away from school for several weeks may need to be given an individualised work programme to allow for 'catching up' and regaining momentum in learning. In responding to pupils' diverse learning needs, the aim is to provide equal opportunity for all children, regardless of gender, race or disability, by motivating them to work hard, making regular assessments of their progress and setting appropriate targets for learning. Particular care needs to be paid to communicating effectively with children for whom English is an additional language. In such cases, strategies include the use of steady, well articulated speech, employing a good range of tactile experiences and making a special effort to involve all the children in creative activities where spoken language is not essential to complete the work. As some children from difficult backgrounds may be frustrated by their inability to conform and contribute to classroom discussion, enlisting the help of a sympathetic child (a 'buddy') to help them adjust, and the close involvement of teaching assistants who possess appropriate language skills, are significant strategies. It is also important to be aware of the potential value of support agencies, such as social services and the educational psychologist, even if you don't have direct contact with them.

There is a difference between high and unreasonable expectations

All teachers want their pupils to do well. However, in the drive for higher standards it is easy to imagine that there is no end to what can be achieved, with the result that children are pressured and cajoled too much, and made the victims of teachers' anxieties. Genuine achievement should be recognised and acknowledged. Children should, of course, be congratulated and praised when they make genuine progress, and encouraged to do better; this is different from a classroom ethos in which good is never good enough, and children despair of ever satisfying their teacher's insatiable demands for more. As you strive to improve the teaching-and-learning climate, Kyriacou's advice that a relaxed, warm and supportive ethos is an important component (Kyriacou 1991).

Keynote: To establish sensible targets for learning.

Motivation is a key factor in high achievement

Some pupils have a strong sense of self-motivation; others require careful directing and a degree of coercion. Teachers lives would be much easier if every child were highly motivated, but this is rarely the case. Your job is to develop an atmosphere in which success is celebrated and children become so involved and interested in what they are doing that they will strive for high standards. In the meantime, and for those pupils who are relatively unmotivated or have a passive attitude towards achievement, you need to define your own expectations in such a way that pupils can have no doubt over what is expected. Sometimes this means spelling them out item by item; for instance, see Table 10.

Keynote: To help pupils develop a sense of pride in their work.

It is not easy to define high expectation

Although the principle of high expectations is one that every teacher would espouse, it is not always easy to know what it looks like in respect of individual pupils. You may suspect that children are capable of more, but if they are underachieving, either due to laziness, indifference or lack of motivation, you may not be sure of what they can do if they try hard. Some children are skilled in convincing teachers that they can only achieve a limited amount when in fact they could do much better. Others lack the confidence and self-esteem to make full use of their abilities. Part of your task as a teacher is to find out the truth by observing closely, encouraging children to aim high and praising genuine effort.

Keynote: To learn what individual pupils are capable of achieving.

Table 10 Specific expectations for written work

- Write your work in draft form initially without worrying over-much about spelling and punctuation
- Read your work to a trusted friend or the teacher
- Make alterations to your draft as a result of reading it aloud
- With the assistance of a partner if necessary, check spelling, punctuation and grammar
- Show your work to the teacher for a final check
- Write up the work neatly on one side of the paper only, putting your name in the top left-hand corner, the date in the top right-hand corner, the title at the top of the page in the centre, then leave two lines of space before you begin writing
- Leave one line of space between each paragraph
- Do not illustrate your work with pictures but add a few touches with coloured pencils (not felt pens) if you wish
- Leave a line of space at the end of your writing and draw a full line across the page
- On the back of the sheet, write a few sentences about how well you think you did this work, and anything you found difficult
- Ask a sensible friend or the teacher to read the final version and tell you what they think about it
- Place the finished work carefully in the 'Finished' box on the teacher's desk

Expectations are also subject to differentiation

The five-year-old who manages to write her own name after much perseverance may well deserve congratulating, despite the reversed letters and the sloping script, and regardless of the fact that her classmate learned to write her name when she was three and is now getting on well with joined-up writing. Expectations for the first girl will clearly be different from those for the second. The first girl will need to be encouraged in correct letter formation, whereas the second girl will need to practise hand control before she can write her name without lifting the pencil from the paper. Similarly, expectations for the eleven-year-old boy who has always struggled with spelling cannot be compared with those for his friend who seems to be a walking dictionary! As children grow older, they are increasingly conscious of their own shortcomings and will cease to try if they feel that the teacher is being patronising or asking the impossible. If you want the best from your pupils, it is necessary to be honest with them about their difficulties but to convince them that they can, with your support, achieve something to be proud of.

Keynote: To modify expectations depending upon the individual.

Expectations are not only academic

All teachers are involved with helping to develop the 'whole person', not merely improving academic attainment. One of your tasks as a teacher is to be explicit about what you expect to see in terms of behaviour, attitudes and diligence. Ensuring that pupils are not deprived of their full education on the base of gender, race or culture is a principle that should be enshrined on every teacher's heart. This is not, however, the same as saying that all children should be treated in the same way. Pupils differ in personality, inclination, experience and ability, and wise teachers build on their strengths and try to compensate for their weaknesses. There is little point in producing educated monsters.

Keynote: To expect high moral standards.

Linguistic disadvantage takes many forms

Some children struggle to communicate because of physical factors (such as crooked teeth), emotional factors (such as unhappy experiences with adults), dialects which differ from the majority of pupils (due to moving from another part of the country), home background (and low-level conversations), country of origin (struggling with English as an additional language), social pressures (such as the perceived need to speak casually to gain acceptability with other pupils), or psychological factors (such as particular forms of autism). Teachers are sometimes uncertain whether to correct children's speech or encourage them to talk more freely. You need to exercise discretion in such matters: on the one hand to acknowledge and accept diversity; on the other hand, to assist pupils to improve their communicative competence through promoting effective speaking and listening. Seek advice from experienced colleagues if uncertain. Make it a rule that you will never tease children because of their dialect or accent.

Keynote: To be aware of communicative weaknesses and ways to make allowance for them.

Many children are caught between cultures

Although we use the term 'culture' to describe particular groups of people, their lifestyles, ideals and (in some cases) religious affiliations, it is important to understand that children live in a multicultural world. Many pupils are caught between the varying expectations of parents, friends, teachers and others in the general community. Although some children may thrive on diversity, it can be difficult for others to know exactly where their loyalties lie and you may observe instances of frustration and depression as a result. You have a role to play in showing that you value the distinctive personality and contribution of each child.

Keynote: To seek ways of celebrating cultural diversity.

We need to be realistic about how much one teacher can cope with

Society has high expectations of schools, but teachers cannot compensate for every family deficiency and personality trait. By helping pupils to learn effectively, and by demonstrating that you value all their endeavours, you can help to provide them with a platform for achieving academic success and establishing their place in the world. The extent to which children make effective use of those opportunities is, however, largely out of your hands, so do not become enmeshed in guilt.

Keynote: To do the best job possible.

Competence check

- ❑ I have established my expectations for pupils' achievement
- ❑ I have communicated those expectations to the children
- ❑ I am taking a positive view of the diversity existing within the class

TMS12 Provide opportunities to develop pupils' wider understanding by relating their learning to real and work-related examples

What you need to take account of...

Reality is a moveable commodity

The things that are unreal today become possibilities tomorrow. The pace of technological advance is so great that almost anything seems within reach. The science-fiction comics of a post-war era look tame compared with the amazing progress of recent years. Pupils' approaches to problem-solving situations and their ideas about future innovations have been influenced by the world around them and you must try to keep abreast of the world as they perceive it if you are to understand how children think and feel.

Keynote: To keep pace with events.

Work-related examples must still be appropriate to children's conceptual development

There has been a strong move in recent years towards making the work done in school vocationally orientated, drawing on children's knowledge gained outside school as a means of extending and enhancing their own, and their classmates' understanding of the wider world. Many teachers encourage children to bring items relating to that world into school (unless their father is a lion tamer!) and telling their friends about things they have learned. Children watch television programmes and read magazines about differing aspects of knowledge and you may be surprised how much they know if given opportunity to tell. It is also worth remembering that tomorrow's workforce will need to be more adaptable than ever before. Most people will change job at least three or four times. Communication skills, working as a member of a team and individually, use of ICT and the ability to meet strict deadlines will be essential elements of many jobs. You can, and should, assist children in preparing for, and coping with, such a world.

Keynote: To start from the pupils' experience about the world.

The future is unknown but some things never alter

In the 1970s, we were being told that the future would consist of a very short working week and lots of leisure time. It was essential, we were reliably informed, to learn new hobbies, take up sports and find interests with which we could while away the hours. What happened?! You have to be careful that you are not carried away with predicting a world in which ICT dominates lives to such an extent that people will remain in their home, shopping only via the Internet, communicating only via electronic mail and learning solely by means of video-conferencing from the comfort of their own armchair. Some of these trends are already visible and will no doubt continue, but it is important that in our haste to prepare children for such an envisaged world, we do not forget that people are basically gregarious, and that family and community life lies at the heart of a civilised society.

Keynote: To keep a sense of proportion in a changing world.

Competence check

- ❑ My lessons help pupils to come to terms with reality without losing the innocence of childhood
- ❑ My lessons incorporate a sufficient number of real examples
- ❑ I am making a satisfactory distinction between absolutes and opinions

CHAPTER 4

Special Educational Needs (SEN1–3)

Special educational needs (SEN) are governed by legislation, notably the Code of Practice (DfES 2001). There are three principal areas with which you must comply:

SEN1 Familiarity with the Code of Practice and individual education plans (IEPs) .

SEN2 Taking account of children who are not fluent in speaking English.

SEN3 Identifying and responding to very able pupils.

SEN1 Familiarity with using the Code of Practice on the identification and assessment of SEN and keeping records on IEPs

What you need to take account of...

SEN has first to be identified

Pupils have special educational needs if they are identified as having learning difficulties which are so distinctive from children of a similar age that they call for special provision to be made. The learning difficulty may be due to low academic ability in the case of able-bodied children or a disability which hinders access to, or use of, educational opportunities. Thus, disabled children may have the same intellectual ability as their able-bodied peers but make slower progress due to the practicalities of daily living, such as the lack of suitable wheelchair access or an inability to communicate verbally. Children must not be regarded as having a learning difficulty solely on the basis of their first language being other than English. The earlier that special educational needs can be identified, the more quickly educational provision can be provided. The Code of Practice provides full details of the responsibilities of schools towards children with special educational needs but you need only have a broad grasp of its contents.

The role of support staff for children with disabilities is crucial to enhance learning through appropriate access to the curriculum (see Mackinnon 2002).

Keynote: To be clear about what constitutes special educational needs.

SEN also includes more able pupils

An intelligent and capable child may be struggling to learn for a variety of reasons. This underachievement is just as significant to the children and parents concerned as those who struggle due to other learning difficulties. Additionally, although there may not be many children in the 'more able' category, you can be fairly certain that there will be at least one case in every class. Some high ability children seem unexceptional when you first meet them. They get on with their work in much the same way as their classmates and do their best to complete the tasks to the teacher's satisfaction. However, they often excel in using imagination and problem solving if given opportunity. They are characterised by an ability to speculate, raise unanticipated questions and show an immense appetite for learning if well motivated. Consequently, they absorb information rapidly and understand the implications of events where other children fail to do so, by 'reading between the lines' of a situation. If under-stimulated or forced to comply with a narrow curriculum, gifted children may exhibit considerable restlessness and show a degree of disaffection or behave badly. They need to have their energies channelled into tasks and activities appropriate to their capability, particularly ones that allow for them to explore ideas, demonstrate initiative and, on occasions, work independently (see also SEN3).

Keynote: To be aware of the full range of pupils' abilities.

Every school has to have an SEN policy

Governing bodies of all maintained schools must publish the school's SEN policy and report annually to parents who have children formally identified as needing special support. There is also one person in every school who acts as the special educational needs coordinator (SENCO) and deals with the day-to-day operation of the policy, liaises with colleagues and gives advice where necessary, and coordinates the special provision. All staff are entitled to receive some training about how to deal more effectively with children who have been designated as having special needs. You should ensure that you know who the SENCO is and learn the basic structure of his or her responsibility. In particular, you should be familiar with the mechanism for liaising with the SENCO about your concerns for individual children. Head teachers, in consultation with the SENCO, have to complete forms to indicate how many children are designated as having a special educational need, so accurate information and good communication between teachers and the SENCO about the children is essential.

Keynote: To liaise with the SENCO.

Following the Code of Practice does not, of itself, improve a situation

The Code of Practice and its associated strategies do not provide a blueprint for success. With every good intention and any amount of hard work, some children do not respond as hoped and seem set to struggle for a long time to come. For example, the provision of Individual Education Plans (IEPs) is helpful if there is the time, resourcing and determination to persevere with them and stay on top of the job, but in reality there is no guarantee that they will achieve what is hoped for. Goals have to be established and monitored on the understanding that there are few short-term solutions for deeply entrenched problems. However, it has been shown that active intervention at an early age can, and often does, offset the impact of learning difficulties, providing both child and parents are included in the discussions and establishment of a plan of action. The Code of Practice does at least ensure that pupils do not slip through the net for years, only to be diagnosed towards the end of primary schooling when intervention is much more difficult.

Keynote: To use every means to assist the less able.

IEPs have to be carefully managed

The IEP should be based on the curriculum that all the other pupils in the class are following, making use of available resources, activities and assessments, and should, as far as possible, form part of the normal classroom setting. It should set out the nature of the learning difficulty, the intended action, how parents can help at home, and some idea of achievement targets. There should be reference in the IEP to monitoring and assessment of the programme, including review arrangements. The review focuses on the effectiveness of the programme and, where possible, involves parents in decisions about whether to draw up a further plan or, where the situation appears to be deteriorating, call upon external expertise. You will not have to manage these procedures but need to be aware of how IEPs are written and how their effectiveness is monitored.

Keynote: To be familiar with the production and monitoring of IEPs.

Special educational needs in the areas of literacy and numeracy are most serious

Children may be poor at running, hopeless at art and confused about scientific principles, and it will probably not have a major deleterious effect upon their lives. If, however, they cannot read and write, or deal competently with number bonds, their education will be blighted. This is why most effort is put into ensuring that all possible help is given to children who are failing to make adequate progress in these areas. Schools are now under considerable pressure from the government to improve standards of literacy and numeracy. Inspections of schools also include the work of students and (in particular) NQTs, so there is no hiding place! This is not to say, of course, that non-core subjects are unimportant. On the contrary, the arts and humanities are often an effective medium for capturing and maintaining children's interest and enthusiasm for learning. Furthermore, there are numerous opportunities for enhancing numeracy and (particularly) literacy skills during topic or project work. Don't make the mistake of believing children are helped by receiving a constant diet of formal, desk-bound tasks. A survey of effective schools (Ofsted 2002) found that high standards of achievement in core subjects are frequently accompanied by an emphasis on imaginative teaching in the humanities, PE and the arts, though these were sometimes taught after the end of the formal school day.

Keynote: To concentrate on pupils' literacy.

Competence check

- ❑ I am familiar with the Code of Practice and children with special educational needs
- ❑ I am liaising with the SENCO
- ❑ My lessons are taking sufficient account of pupils' needs

SEN2 Take account of children who are not fluent in English in lesson planning and delivery

What you need to take account of...

Delivery and vocabulary needs to be appropriate

Some inexperienced teachers are prone to speak too quickly or indistinctly, especially when they get excited. If you have pupils for whom English is an additional language (EAL) in the class or group, pay special attention to your diction, pace of speech and phrasing. All children require time to absorb what a teacher says; this is especially true if English is not their native tongue. In particular, you will need to be explicit and careful when using subject-specific vocabulary, casual expressions or colloquialisms. On the other hand, recognise that such pupils will be familiar with the idioms and phrases commonly used by children of their age. Knowing how to explain complex issues using straightforward terminology is a priority for every teacher.

Keynote: To verbally communicate effectively.

All pupils should be given appropriately challenging work

Children are not unintelligent simply because the first language they speak at home happens to be different from that used by the teachers in school. It is important not to underestimate the ability of EAL children and allocate unsuitable or mundane tasks (see also P3). Careful explanations and close monitoring are particularly important during the first part of the lesson. Relationships between teacher and taught are especially significant for children who are not fluent in English as they will often need to confirm and check that what they are doing is correct. Many EAL children struggle at first due to the extra communication demands made upon them. If they are placed with a sympathetic and patient child who will help them through the vagaries of the system during the first few weeks in school and given full access to activities in which speech is not wholly essential (such as games and computers) the majority of children quickly settle and fit in. Younger and more vulnerable children will require sympathetic handling, but still need gradual exposure to all aspects of school life. Children with EAL will sometimes require the help of a classroom assistant or language specialist but this does not signify that they are intellectually dull.

Keynote: To recognise the ability and potential of every child.

Some children receive additional support

As part of your planning, you may need to take account of the additional support that a pupil or group of pupils receive. In doing so, check when the support person is available and whether the child receives additional help inside or outside the classroom. If a number of children are classified as coming from New Commonwealth countries, extra support is sometimes provided through a Section 11 teacher. If children go outside the classroom to receive extra support, you will need to take account of the potential distraction when they return and have to be re-integrated into the lesson. Liaison with support staff is very important and has to be taken into account in terms of the time and effort it requires.

Keynote: To acknowledge the work of additional support staff.

Lesson planning should incorporate speaking and listening activities

Children for whom English is an additional language require regular opportunities to speak and listen, using tape recordings, computer-generated speech or, best of all, other children (see also TMS8). A lot of children are shy or reluctant to speak to adults but may be willing to talk to their peers. It is important to note that some children from other cultures may have been used to having a different relationship with their teachers from the majority of your class. This can lead to over-zealous or unacceptable behaviour for a time until the children have absorbed the classroom norms. You will also need to have a lot of patience and persistence with new some pupils who may, on occasions, use their ignorance to exploit the situation.

Keynote: To structure opportunities for speaking and listening.

Competence check

❑ I am careful in the way that I speak, pronounce words and introduce vocabulary
❑ I am ensuring that all children are involved in work appropriate to their ability
❑ I am taking sufficient account of pupils' additional language needs

SEN3 Identify and respond appropriately to very able pupils

What you need to take account of...

Able children may be inconspicuous

As noted in SEN1, not every able child stands out immediately from the rest of the class. Sometimes, the passive child who produces unimaginative written work may prove to have a surprisingly strong grasp of difficult concepts and be capable of solving demanding problems in innovative ways. Some able children are slow of speech and thought, yet far exceed their peers in their understanding of complex issues. Because of large class sizes, it is possible to overlook able children and judge them solely on their visible output. Teare (1997) suggests that able and talented pupils include those who score highly on intelligence tests, but also those who demonstrate outstanding talent in areas as diverse as sporting ability, music, drama and design. He argues that creativity, leadership and organisational qualities, mechanical ingenuity and other human abilities may be signals that a child is able. He also offers a list of criteria by which you can recognise talented and able pupils (see Table 11).

Keynote: To be alert to the existence of special abilities.

Table 11 Characteristics of able and talented children (based on Teare 1997)

- Superior powers of reasoning
- Originality and initiative
- Ability to absorb and classify information
- Detects weaknesses in others, including adults
- Unusually high personal standards
- Absorbed for long periods of time in matters of great personal interest and resents interruption

Able children may be conspicuous

Not all able children are inconspicuous. Some of them are quickly identifiable due to their willingness to answer questions, volunteer for difficult tasks and take responsibility for group activities. Able children are often resourceful, imaginative and hungry for work. They can absorb large amounts of information, search out a variety of facts, complete pages of work, and still come back for more. Many are eager to do well, competent in most areas of the curriculum and popular with their peers. Able children are frequently characterised by their ability to hold sophisticated conversations with adults and incorporate their experiences from outside school into their daily work. Your positive and affirming responses are as necessary for this group of children as any other.

Keynote: To celebrate the talent and enthusiasm of able pupils.

Able children may be restless spirits

All children can be restless at times, but some of the very able children may find it difficult to settle to regular work. Such children wander about the room, poking into the library, commenting on what might appear to be trivial bits of knowledge that they have gleaned from different sources. Sometimes they prefer to work alone and spend excessive amounts of time on a narrowly focused activity in order to satisfy their thirst for mental engagement. You may be tempted (quite understandably) to give these non-conformists some straightforward tasks to keep them tied down; however, if you can present them with a variety of problem-solving tasks which hold their interest and stretch their intellects, you will soon find out whether the child is truly able or just lacking the ability to concentrate.

Keynote: To focus intellectual energy into purposeful activities.

Able children need to be valued

Although they excel in some aspects of academic work, very able children are as diverse as other groups of children in terms of how good their aptitude for sport, their preferences, hobbies and interests are. Able children may be emotionally immature or quite sophisticated. Whatever their personal characteristics, you should treat them in a way that is appropriate to their ages and not as alien beings who inhabit the school planet! Able children also need encouragement and praise. It is surprisingly easy to 'let them get on with it' or to minimise their achievements by giving the impression that as they have a good brain they do not deserve credit for anything. Part of your task is to value effort and achievement for every child at every level.

Keynote: To enthuse about all achievement.

Extreme ability may gain a child popularity or scorn

Many able children are popular with their peers, especially if they are willing to share their expertise and be helpful during lessons. However, if able children are perceived as slightly odd or are socially immature, they may attract unwelcome attention, disregard or bullying. It has been known for able children to underachieve as a means of maintaining friendships which they might otherwise have forfeited. It is part of your responsibility to develop a culture of learning with your pupils, such that achievement and the application of mental ability or other skills are seen as positive attributes rather than oddities. Children have to be shown that serious work and achievement can be just as much fun as messing about with trivial activities.

Keynote: To foster a work culture.

Ability goes beyond the school curriculum

Some children are quite expert in areas not covered by the curriculum, such as hobbies developed at home, interests shared with a parent or a passion that has grown through the years. In addition, there are many children who, though they never excel academically, are exceptional in terms of their caring ways, sincerity, endeavour and friendly disposition. If you show enthusiasm about the things that children value, and make a point of allowing them to share their achievements with others, you will discover their many hidden talents. Once you have demonstrated to your pupils that effort, diligence and perseverance in situations outside the school curriculum are also worth celebrating, success quickly becomes infectious.

Keynote: To celebrate every form of determined effort.

Competence check

- ❑ I have identified pupils with special abilities
- ❑ I have made adequate provision for their needs in my planning
- ❑ I am developing a culture of success among my pupils

CHAPTER 5

Assessment (A1–7)

The role of assessment in learning has been highlighted over recent years. Assessment is located within the overall process of monitoring, assessing, recording, reporting and accountability, MARRA (Headington 2000). You need to demonstrate your competence in seven key areas:

A1 Assessing learning objectives as a means of improving planning and teaching.
A2 Marking and monitoring progress.
A3 Recording pupils' progress as a means of improving their learning.
A4 Assessing pupils against attainment targets.
A5 Familiarity with level descriptions and end-of-key-stage descriptions.
A6 Using different kinds of assessment appropriately.
A7 Using assessment data to establish learning targets for pupils.

A1 Assess how well learning objectives have been achieved and use this assessment to improve planning and teaching

What you need to take account of...

Assessments can be random or specific

The majority of teacher assessments are gained randomly as they notice pupils' behaviour and attitudes, hear them making comments about the work, see the written outputs they produce and pick up snippets of other relevant information. Some assessments are more structured, especially information gained through question and answer, responses to tasks, and discussion groups. Some assessments are highly structured when information about pupils' learning is gained through test conditions and formal marking criteria.

Keynote: To be aware of different assessment opportunities.

The best assessments influence planning

Assessment of pupils' progress is not merely to provide information to put on a record card or in a school report but to assist in lesson preparation. There are three aspects of assessment that you can use: (i) specific errors made by pupils in their answers to questions or written work which indicate misunderstanding or limited grasp of the issues (ii) incorrect answers made during reinforcement activities which show that basic concepts need revising; (iii) pupils' mastery of skills and concepts which provide evidence that it is time to introduce more advanced work. The third of these is particularly important as assessment is sometimes viewed as ways of discovering pupil failings rather than pupil successes. Consequently, assessment has acquired a negative image which it hardly deserves. Once you see assessment as a means of enhancing your teaching and learning, you will never be short of material for future lessons.

Keynote: To use assessment constructively.

Learning objectives and learning outcomes may differ

However carefully you design your lessons, you cannot guarantee that the children will learn what you intend them to, or that you will discover precisely what they have learned. Teaching and learning rarely follows a simple progression from planning to teaching to outcomes to assessment. Because the children were all listening to you at the same time and engaged on identical or similar tasks, it does not mean that they have learned the same things. As it is impossible to assess every child during every session, it is useful to select a few 'target' children and examine the evidence for their learning more closely to act as a yardstick for the class as a whole. You can change the children that you target from time to time to get a more complete picture. The more specific you can be about what you hope the children learn (or begin to learn) the more you will be able to evaluate what is happening and use the assessment information gained to plan future lessons, but it would be a mistake to believe that it is a seamless process.

Keynote: To monitor learning outcomes.

Assessment does not necessarily improve learning

You can spend a lot of time pouring over samples of children's work, talking to them about what they should have learned and applying a battery of formal tests, but they will not of themselves make a great deal of difference unless you scrutinise the evidence and think through the implications for your own lesson planning. Some inexperienced teachers spend precious time compiling fancy lists of assessment results which, though they may look very impressive, have a limited impact on their classroom performance or the way they organise learning. Unless assessment and recording has a positive impact on teaching effectiveness, you may as well save yourself the trouble.

Keynote: To spend assessment time wisely.

Pupils can give helpful information

Take note of what the children say about your lessons. Watch how enthusiastic they are to do more of the same. Listen for their comments as they leave the room. Read their body language. If possible, find out directly through casual questioning of some key pupils how they perceived the lesson and what they made of it. The best lessons may not always be the most popular with pupils, but they are usually characterised by a notable increase in children's verbal responsiveness.

Keynote: To encourage self-assessment.

Competence check

- ❑ My lesson evaluation incorporates assessment of learning objectives
- ❑ I am using a variety of sources to gain an overall impression of lesson success
- ❑ I am using information from one lesson to guide my detailed planning for future lessons

A2 Mark and monitor work, provide constructive oral and written feedback and set targets for pupils' progress

What you need to take account of...

Marking has time and practical implications

Marking is usually a slow business if carried out thoroughly (see P3 and TMS10). For instance, if you have thirty Year 6 essays to mark at home, it will take you at least four hours to complete. Similarly, marking pages and pages of mathematical computations is an exhausting task. Some work requires no more than a cursory glance to ensure that it has been completed. Some can be marked by pupils themselves. Other work needs to be taken and marked away from the classroom. The majority of work should, ideally, be marked during the lesson with the pupils present or as soon after the teaching event as possible. You have to decide whether the time taken in marking is justified in terms of the value to children's learning. Sometimes you will only want to mark a specific aspect of work and ignore others. Be aware, however, that a parent looking at the marked work may be puzzled that you have overlooked errors.

Keynote: To clarify the purpose of marking.

Decide whether written or oral feedback is best

A lot of monitoring can be undertaken through speaking to the pupils concerned and providing constructive suggestions, asking searching (but non-threatening) questions and involving other children in providing ideas and suggestions about appropriate methods or solutions. Written feedback is far more time consuming and, with the best will in the world, usually consists of only a few words. Although children like to see comments such as 'Well done, you have worked hard' on their work, these are more to encourage than to assess the quality. Children will make most progress when they take careful note of your feedback and are encouraged to persevere by your response. A lot of red pen across the page damages pupils' self-esteem.

Keynote: To provide appropriate feedback.

Involve the pupils in setting targets

The expression 'target setting' can invoke a lot of anxiety among teachers. However, it is simply a way of helping pupils to move from their current position of understanding and capability to a more secure or advanced one. Most targets can be set by talking to the pupils concerned and pointing out how things might be improved. Many children are acutely aware of the need for improvement and are anxious to do so. They may be less clear about the standard they need to reach and strategies for achieving it. Part of your role as a teacher is to provide guidance in helping them do so (see Pascal and Bertram 1997 for early years case studies in improvement). It may be appropriate to encourage children to keep their own records of progress by providing them with a list of 'I can do...' items relevant to the topic or subject area that they can tick for themselves (Clemson and Clemson 1996).

Keynote: To involve pupils in their learning.

Homework should not become burdensome

With the increased attention paid to the importance of homework in raising standards, it is tempting to place too much emphasis upon it and create something of a monster that absorbs too much of your time and attention, and makes too many demands upon young children (see also P3 and TMS10). Homework should be easy to administer and monitor. Where possible, pupils and parents should take the major responsibility for the administration (such as marking reading records); your task is to incorporate elements of the work into mainstream classwork. If you find that setting and marking homework detracts from your principal responsibilities for the daily teaching-and-learning programme, you need to reduce its priority rating.

Keynote: To use homework to support teaching and learning.

Competence check

- ❑ I am following the school's and class teacher's marking policy
- ❑ I am monitoring and marking work in a way that assists pupils' learning
- ❑ I am using information from monitoring and marking to help shape my lesson planning

A3 Assess and record each pupil's progress systematically, using focused observation, questioning, testing and marking

Use these records effectively to:

1. check that pupils have understood and completed the work set;
2. monitor strengths and weaknesses and use the information gained as a basis for purposeful intervention in pupils' learning;
3. inform planning;
4. check that pupils continue to make demonstrable progress in their acquisition of the knowledge, skills and understanding of the subject.

What you need to take account of...

Assessing and recording for every pupil is a major task

The description contained within this standard may lead teachers to attempt the impossible task of providing individual curricula for every pupil. Even experienced teachers find it difficult to keep pace with every pupil's progress in each key area of the curriculum. Maintaining records which accurately reflect children's understanding, strengths and weaknesses is based on the assumption that all progress is quantifiable and has led to teachers wasting a considerable amount of time in endlessly ticking, colouring and annotating records and lists. It is only worth filling in a record if it is useful in one of two ways: either it gives information to help colleagues and parents understand their children's progress or it helps you to reflect more purposefully on ways of improving learning.

Keynote: To maintain essential records.

There must be valid and reliable methods of testing

Any form of test must take account of two things: its validity and its reliability. A test has to be valid in that the results are a true reflection of a pupil's knowledge, understanding or skill level in an area of learning. For instance, if you are testing ten-year-olds' ability to read and interpret instructions, it would be valid to use a sample of writing based on (say) a design and technology project on which the class had recently been engaged, but invalid to use text from a book on quantum mechanics, about which the pupils were completely unfamiliar. Similarly, it would be valid to test pupils' understanding of number bonds if they were presented in a conventional form (base-10), but invalid if children were suddenly given sums in base-5! The extent of a test's reliability can be found in whether the results can be replicated through further, similar tests. For instance, some children are coached by parents just prior to starting school and may thereby achieve an inflated score; if, after a lapse of ten days or so, the same test yielded markedly different results, we might suspect that the test was unreliable for the coached group of children, though reliable for the others. Reliability, then, has to take account of the conditions under which the test is given and the circumstances influencing the outcome. Thus, if children have to take an examination in an unfamiliar place with teachers they have never met, their results may not reflect their ability due to their insecurity; in such a case, we would probably feel justified in claiming that the results were unreliable even if the test itself was valid.

Keynote: To take account of validity and reliability of tests.

Focused observation requires planning

In a busy primary classroom, it is normally impossible to spend any length of time observing a single pupil. To do so requires particular forms of planning: giving the class a task which will keep pupils busily occupied to minimise demands upon yourself; using a classroom assistant or fellow teacher to take the major responsibility for the class while you record your judgements; organising lessons in such a way that the target children are engaged in tasks which provide the sort of information you are looking for. It is not possible to observe everything at once and it is sensible to select two or three specific areas of learning or behaviour for special attention. For instance, you might be interested in seeing how independently children work, the length of their attention span, their application to the task or their use of equipment. You may, on the other hand, wish to note how often they interrupt others, support their partners, offer verbal contributions or write down ideas. As part of any focused observation, you will also want to ask fundamental questions about the quality of work produced by paying attention to whether the task was well matched to the child and the impact of the organisation for learning (Wragg 1994).

Keynote: To organise for observing.

Written records are only a snapshot in time

However rapidly you complete a record sheet after assessing progress, it will always be out of date. Young children, in particular, will make sudden spurts in their learning which confound your earlier assessments; others will appear to have grasped something, only for you to find that they did not understand it so well after all. It is simply not possible for teachers to constantly update record cards, so they will inevitably show an incomplete picture. Most up-to-date records of pupils' progress have to be kept in your head until the important points can be written down.

Keynote: To keep the usefulness of records in perspective.

Records of Achievement are valuable sources of information

Since the introduction of the National Curriculum, many schools have introduced a system of files or folders in which aspects of a pupil's work, skills, abilities and personal qualities are acknowledged. Primary schools often include a portfolio of each child's work, in which samples from different areas of the curriculum are included. Mitchell and Koshy (1995) suggest that a good Record of Achievement will recognise that children learn at different speeds and that their abilities and development are not fixed. It helps children to reflect carefully about the quality of their work as they select, with teacher support, samples to be included in the folder. A concentration of positive achievements can also be a spur to self-confidence and success. If you are involved in helping children to select from their repertoire for inclusion in the folder, you may be surprised at some of their choices (which will be different from your own). The process of selection does give opportunity for you to talk to the children about their work and discuss standards. Any work included in the folder should contain the date of completion and some brief details concerning the level of support the child received.

Keynote: To use Records of Achievement as a spur to progress.

Competence check

- ❑ My records provide useful and usable information about the progress of individuals
- ❑ I have based my decisions about progress on a range of evidence sources
- ❑ I have a clearer understanding of individual pupils' knowledge and understanding after assessing and recording than I did before

A4 Assess pupils' progress against attainment targets with guidance from an experienced teacher

What you need to take account of...

Attainment targets are guides to achievement

The eight level descriptions describe the types and range of performance that pupils working at a particular level should characteristically demonstrate. From time to time it is a useful exercise to practise matching samples of children's work in mathematics, English and science with the appropriate National Curriculum descriptors to get a feel for the standards at different levels. Although attainment targets provide a useful measure of pupils' progress, they are neither infallible nor absolute. They offer one means of assessing achievement by providing a 'best fit' for pupil attainment. They should not be dismissed as irrelevant or elevated beyond their usefulness. Unfortunately, because they have assumed such a high profile in gauging teaching effectiveness and reporting to parents, they tend to be thought of as the final word rather than one indicator among many.

Keynote: To use levels of achievement as one guide to pupils' progress.

There are national compulsory tests and tasks during primary schooling

Tests and tasks are given to all children at the end of Key Stages 1 and 2. Tests are in areas where it is possible to give a numerical score; tasks require teacher assessment and moderation by teachers in different schools. The two Standard Assessment Tasks (SATs) cover the following areas:

- Year 2 children: reading, writing (including handwriting), spelling and mathematics;
- Year 6 children: reading, writing (including handwriting), spelling, mathematics, mental arithmetic and science.

Keynote: To be aware of national requirements.

SATs form the heart of formal assessment

The SATs are the most notable example of determining attainment levels. Head teachers receive details of the tasks a few weeks in advance of the time they have to be taken but are not allowed to open them until shortly before they are administered. Teachers of Year 2 usually have to make a considerable effort to organise the tests, normally with the help of another teacher (who may be brought in for this purpose). Once the tests have been completed, some of the answers can be marked using an optical reader; others require marking according to set criteria. The accumulated marks for the different sections of the SATs are collated (sometimes using computer software) and a final level of attainment for mathematics and English is determined. The process is not intended to disrupt the children's education but there are inevitably some undesirable consequences, including preparing children for the tests by 'cramming' and getting children back into a routine once the tests are over. Teachers are also left with the arduous job of transferring the SATs results into a format which parents can understand. Year 6 teachers follow a similar procedure to those of Year 2 pupils, but in their case the tests include science, and the completed test papers are sent away for external marking.

Keynote: To become familiar with procedures for SATs.

Teachers have to provide their own assessments of pupils

Teachers are responsible for assessing pupils' progress through the normal procedures of setting and evaluating work from day to day, together with any in-school tests that may be used to provide a clearer picture of children's progress. Teacher assessments are required for some areas of English, mathematics and science in addition to the formal SATs testing. Key Stage 2 assessments at Levels 1 and 2 are made by the teacher. Teachers of pupils in Years 2 and 6 have to provide their own evidence for levels of attainment, based on comparing pupils' work with that of children of similar age elsewhere by using published guides containing performance descriptions (SCAA 1995). Teachers from the different schools in a locality also bring along samples of work to the forum as a means of monitoring consistency of judgement for samples of English work (especially writing). In practice, teachers tend to wait until the SATs results are available before finally committing themselves to grades for their children. Teacher assessment levels for any one child are frequently identical to the SATs result.

Keynote: To have suitable evidence to carry out teacher assessments.

Levels of achievement are used to compare the success of schools

It is important for you to understand that although the children's progress is of immediate concern to you, there is a wider agenda involving governors, inspectors, local authorities and national education bodies (such as the Qualifications and Curriculum Authority (QCA)) in which results are used to determine the school's success. If results do not meet expectations, head teachers and governors may find themselves criticised by inspectors and, if things do not improve, the school may be placed under close scrutiny until it does so.

Keynote: To be part of a collaborative effort in raising standards.

Competence check

- ❑ I am familiar with the appropriate attainment targets
- ❑ I have concentrated my efforts on ensuring that pupils have a firm grasp of core subjects areas
- ❑ I have taken advice from a more experienced teacher about measuring attainment

A5 Understand what is demanded of pupils in relation to level descriptions and end-of-key-stage descriptions

What you need to take account of...

Level descriptions should not dominate curriculum planning and assessment

It is surprisingly easy to orientate your teaching in such a way that you 'teach to the test' by training children in an unimaginative way rather than allowing them to explore learning and gain important experience about failure and disappointment, giving them the opportunity to modify or redesign particular approaches, and follow instinctive lines of enquiry that lead to learning outcomes which are different from the ones that you originally intended. It is useful to keep your eye on level descriptions but not to allow them to dictate everything you want children to learn.

Keynote: To distinguish between education and training.

End-of-key-stage descriptions only apply to certain subjects

Art, music and PE are assessed using end-of-key-stage descriptions which indicate the type and range of performance that the majority of pupils should characteristically demonstrate by the end of that key stage, assuming that they have been taught the necessary programmes of study. The eight level descriptions are not used for these three subjects.

Keynote: To become familiar with end-of-key-stage descriptions.

Literacy permeates every curriculum area

The ability to read and write is important regardless of the subject being studied. Pupils need to have a firm grasp of literacy and develop the ability to express themselves orally if they are to extend their learning. You need to do all you can to encourage children to develop effective study skills (such as the use of an index, a dictionary and a database) and communication skills (such as the ability to summarise findings, explain things to other pupils, tell a friend how something is done) if they are to make the most of their opportunities. In particular, most good readers are potentially high achievers; whereas poor readers, regardless of how hard you try to motivate them, will tend to underachieve, even in those areas of learning which do not require strong reading ability (see P5 and TMS9).

Keynote: To enhance standards of literacy.

Attainment Target 1 makes particular demands of pupils and teachers

The AT1 for English, mathematics and science in the National Curriculum involves Speaking and Listening, Using and Applying Mathematics and Experimental and Investigative Science, respectively. These areas of the curriculum are quite demanding for teachers to plan as they require a variety of teaching methods to be employed, including, for example, interactive class or group discussion to facilitate speaking and listening skills, and mathematical investigations based on relevant situations. Typically, lessons can be based on the mathematics of building a school extension, plans for the establishment of a new play area, the correct size of hat brim to ensure protection from the effects of the sun, repositioning the classroom furniture to allow for safe access. Science experiments should allow for collaborative planning, design, testing and recording of results in a variety of ways. Lessons in these curriculum areas give you clear insights into children's grasp of skills and concepts.

Keynote: To tackle the curriculum in AT1 with determination.

Competence check

- ❑ I am familiar with the appropriate level descriptions and end-of-key-stage descriptions
- ❑ I have not allowed level descriptions to dominate my planning
- ❑ My lesson planning includes opportunities for pupils in AT1

A6 Use different kinds of assessment appropriately for different purposes

What you need to take account of...

Pupils are assessed on entering school

All pupils aged four or five years, both full and part-time, have to be assessed on admittance to a primary school, unless they are placed in a designated nursery class (QCA 1997). Assessment has to cover aspects of language and literacy, mathematics, and personal and social development, identified through a range of desirable outcomes (see Table 12). Included in the assessment must be one or more quantitative results capable of being used for later 'value-added' analyses (see below). Pupils are assessed by the class teacher within the first half term using information from playgroup leaders, nursery teachers and parents wherever possible about the children's strengths and achievements. In liaison with parents, targets are set for future progress and some arrangements made for future review of progress. Many assessment schemes include details about children's pre-school attendance, free school meal entitlement, ethnic background and special educational needs (Lindsay and Desforges 1998). Assessments must be carried out within the first seven weeks of a child entering school and place heavy time demands upon reception class teachers.

Keynote: To have a clear idea about pupils' current capability.

Table 12 Desirable outcomes for children's learning (SCAA 1997)

- Personal and social development
- Language and literacy
- Mathematics
- Knowledge and understanding of the world
- Physical development
- Creative development

The Foundation Stage has distinctive features

Curriculum Guidance for the Foundation Stage (DfEE 2000a) provides 'stepping stones' of progress towards the early learning goals that help teachers to identify the knowledge, skills, understanding and attitudes that children need to achieve the goals. The stepping stones are not supposed to be age-related but broadly speaking the yellow band applies to three-year-olds, the blue to four-year-olds and the green to five-year-olds. The early learning goals are underpinned by the stepping stones and are organised into six areas of learning, as seen in Table 12. All teachers who work in early childhood settings also need to be familiar with the structure and uses of the *Foundation Stage Profile*, details of which are available on the QCA website: www.qca.org.uk. The use of the term 'profile' is significant, as it reflects an approach to the assessment of young children based on what a child actually knows and is capable of doing with regard to the early learning goals and the foundation curriculum. Assessments do not rely on children taking tasks or completing set tasks, but on the teacher's observations, perceptions and garnering of evidence through regular interaction with the children over a period of time.

Initial assessments provide a marker for future progress

Subsequent progress in reading and number at the end of Key Stage 1 (when the child is aged about seven years) is compared with the baseline assessment. The difference between the scores is known as 'value-added' to indicate the difference that the early years of schooling has made to the child's attainment (Tymms

1996; see also Carr 2001). Schools are expected to ensure that there has been substantial progress during the intervening time. It is not only helpful to know children's current attainment but the rate at which they seem to be improving. The validity of this type of comparison has been called into question. There are also optional tests for Years 3, 4 and 5 available to schools who want to monitor pupils' progress more closely. Schools are not obliged to disclose these results to parents, though many elect to do so. One reason for carrying out baseline assessments is to try to ensure that schools with intakes of low achievers are not unfairly disadvantaged compared with their capable neighbours. It is obvious that children who enter school already well advanced in their academic work are likely to achieve higher results in their Key Stage 1 assessments by the time they are seven. However, with a baseline assessment available, it is claimed that the extent of each child's progress can be calculated more precisely. One advantage of this approach to determining pupils' achievement is that it allows schools with weaker Key Stage 1 SATs results to demonstrate that pupils have made some progress, albeit from a lower starting point, compared with schools in which children come from more advantaged backgrounds. One other reason why it is important for schools to show that pupils are progressing is that the 'value-added' element provides a measure of teaching effectiveness (see Table 13).

Keynote: To measure the extent of pupils' progress.

Table 13 An example of an assessment schema

1. Qualitative statements in the form of a profile are provided by a nursery or reception teacher when the child starts school, together with information from parents (sometimes gained through home visits by teachers from the receiving schools)
2. The reception teacher makes a 'best fit' for the child's present achievements using a graded series of descriptors in the areas of Social and emotional development/ Language/Mathematics
3. Future achievements are compared with the baseline assessment profile to determine the children's progress in number and reading (in particular)

Tests and tasks take time

The tests and tasks are held during the summer term for seven-year-olds, usually spread over several days to avoid undue fatigue. Tests for eleven-year-olds normally take place on set days during May. The SATs for Year 2 children are not intended to take more than three hours in total, and around five hours for Year 6 children. It is important to remember that these are the times that the children actually spend in carrying out the tests and tasks. Teachers have to commit additional time in understanding the requirements, sorting out the tasks, organising for the tests to take place and other administrative demands. If children are absent on the day of the test, separate arrangements need to be made for them to sit it. This in itself causes more work and organisation. The national assessment tests are marked externally. Results are returned to schools in time for their annual reports to parents in which test results have to be disclosed.

Keynote: To take account of tasks and tests in organising teaching.

There are levels of achievement for SATs

Most children in Year 2 should reach at least Level 2 in the tests. Most children in Year 6 should reach at least Level 4. The government is trying to increase the percentage of children achieving these grades and insisting that schools set increasingly higher targets. Very able pupils at the end of Key Stage 1 can be entered for the Key Stage 2, Level 4 tests in reading, writing or mathematics. To allow for variations in children's ages, the raw scores in English reading and spelling tests and the mathematics test at Key Stages 1 and 2 can be adjusted by teachers to give scores which more fairly reflect attainment by making allowance for the considerable differences that may be found in children depending on their date of birth. A separate test for mental arithmetic, lasting some 20 to 30 minutes is now part of the statutory assessment.

Keynote: To understand the expectations for levels of achievement.

Parents are entitled to information about their child's level of attainment

Following statutory assessments, parents have a right to request written information about their child's level of attainment in each attainment target of the core subjects on the National Curriculum 1-8 scale. Head teachers are obliged to provide this information within three weeks (see Table 14 as an example of how a report is structured).

Keynote: To be aware of parental rights.

Assessment results follow the child from school to school

Some children transfer at age seven or eight years to a different school. The sending school has to supply the receiving school with the child's most recent and all previous statutory assessment results in English, mathematics and science. Similarly, when pupils transfer from primary to secondary school, their Key Stage 2 test results will accompany them.

Keynote: To facilitate continuity of assessment.

Table 14 End of Key Stage 1 assessment results: report to parents

Levels of attainment are provided in the following subject areas:

English

- Teacher assessment results in Speaking and Listening/Reading/Writing
- Task and test results in reading task/reading comprehension test/writing task/spelling test

Mathematics

- Teacher assessment result
- Task and test results

Science

- Teacher assessment result
- There are no tasks or tests in science at Key Stage 1

Teachers are under pressure during the time of SATs

Although teachers are becoming more used to managing national tests and tasks, they involve a lot of effort and close cooperation between the teachers involved and the head teacher. Gipps, Brown and McAllister (1995) found that 25 out of 31 school head teachers reported increased levels of stress during the administration of the SATs. Schools with the highest stress levels were those in which there had been a considerable amount of reorganisation and disruption to accommodate the tests. Teachers' anxiety was also found to be due to the high profile that the assessments received and, from Key Stage 1 staff, the need formally to label young children. If you are a student teacher, you need to be aware of the increased pressure on staff during the SATs season and the possible changes to the normal teaching programme which may accompany it. If you are placed with a Year 2 or Year 6 class during their assessment period, you will have to demonstrate flexibility and offer your full support to the teachers involved, regardless of the imposition it makes on your teaching programme. If you are a new teacher, it is unlikely that you will be asked to take a Year 2 or 6 class during your first year, unless you are in a village school with several year groups in the same class.

Keynote: To be especially cooperative during a period of formal assessment.

Competence check

- ❑ I am broadly familiar with the composition of assessments for new school entrants
- ❑ I understand the significance of tasks and tests at the end of key stages
- ❑ I am familiar with the requirements for teacher assessments

A7 Understand and know how national, local, comparative and school data can be used to set clear targets for pupils' achievement

What you need to take account of...

A wide range of data can be used in target setting

To set appropriate targets for pupils, it is important to evaluate a pupil's achievements by reference to a wide range of data to gain an accurate profile of ability and potential (see Figure 7). A child may be top of the class but still underachieving. Another child may be in the middle range of achievements for the class, but doing well or poorly by contrast with similar groups of the same age elsewhere. You have to make a professional judgement about what an individual might achieve, while being sensitive to what realistically can be achieved.

Keynote: To use data constructively.

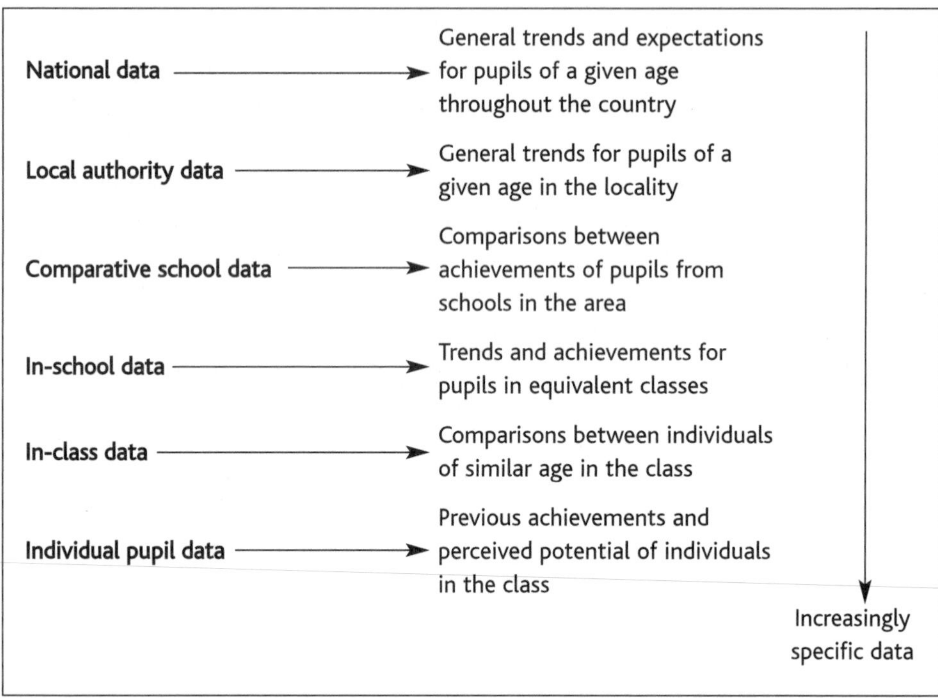

Figure 7 Data for target setting

The SATs results of individual children are confidential

The national tests are an attempt to allow comparisons between the performance of different schools. Schools are obliged to print a summary of their year's SATs results in their brochure for parents, so that they are kept fully informed of the overall picture. However, only the parents or guardians of individual children are entitled to receive the specific information pertaining to their children. You should be careful not to share specific test scores with anyone who does not have a direct professional interest in them. Parents are entitled to see their children's completed task and test papers.

Keynote: To respect confidentiality.

Differences between teacher assessment and test results may have to be explained

In reports to parents, teachers have to provide a brief comment about what the assessment levels indicate about a child's progress. If there are variations between the teacher assessments and results from tasks and tests, some explanation may be needed to justify the differences. For instance, teachers may need to explain that their own assessments are based on a longer-term perspective than the external ones, which provide only a snapshot of a child's understanding at a given time and place.

Keynote: To have appropriate evidence to support teacher assessments.

SATs results do not tell the whole story

Any formal assessment task has to take account of at least six factors. First, some children are frightened by a formal situation and may underachieve due to anxiety. Second, however carefully a test is designed, it will be interpreted differently by different pupils. Third, cultural norms and preferences affect the way in which pupils respond to questions. Fourth, some children have English as an additional language or have poor language skills which may hinder their ability to work rapidly and efficiently. Fifth, tests demand a concentration span of which some pupils are incapable. Sixth, some pupils do not begin their academic growth until they are older and therefore fail to register a satisfactory SATs result in Key Stage 1. Broadfoot (1996) notes that children's achievements are often affected by the learning context itself. Despite the great care that is taken by the QCA to produce tests and tasks that are both valid and reliable, SATs are subject to the same sort of limitations as other tests and should be used alongside your knowledge of the individual needs and potential of the child concerned (Drummond 1993).

Keynote: To put SATs results into perspective.

Schools keep samples of work of equivalent standard to the different National Curriculum levels of attainment

Many schools have a large book with samples of children's work in core subjects to indicate the sort of work which is equivalent to a particular standard. Class teachers will have samples of children's work with an indication of the conditions under which the work was carried out and the teachers' assessment of its quality.

Keynote: To examine typical samples of children's work at different levels.

Competence check

- ❑ I am aware of the need to set appropriate targets for learning
- ❑ I understand that a profile of a child's achievements relies both on the teacher's assessment and the standard tasks and tests
- ❑ I take test and task results into account when planning lessons and series of lessons

CHAPTER 6

Reporting (R1)

Assessment, recording and reporting to parents tend to be inter-related. However, there is one specific standard relating solely to reporting:

R1 Knowing how to prepare and present informative reports to parents and colleagues

What you need to take account of...

Most schools actively encourage parents to make contributions to school development

Gone are the days when schools had a sign saying 'No parents past this point'. In today's consumer climate and with the extent of accountability demanded of head teachers and governors, parents are represented through the appointment of at least one parent governor and a variety of other means. For instance, some schools canvass parents before taking important decisions; others set up open forums or take samples of parental opinion. Inspectors take careful note of the seriousness with which schools treat parental opinion. A school may face severe criticism if it has taken insufficient account of parents' views. Parents are one of the most powerful voices in education. You should take every opportunity to develop a friendly, professional relationship with them (see *FPT*, Chapter 3).

Keynote: To value parental contributions to learning.

Schools are not always willing or able to involve students in the reporting process

If you are still in the early stages of training, you may find that some teachers are quite nervous about allowing you to have access to parents for fear that you might say or do something to the detriment of the class or school. Other teachers encourage and expect you to have regular informal contact with parents, but draw the line at anything formal. Very few schools allow students to write formal comments about pupils to send to parents, though the teacher responsible for the class or group will value receiving some information from you about pupils' progress that can be incorporated into the record system for future use. You may need to arrange with your mentor an opportunity to offer your written comments to a 'surrogate' parent (perhaps another teacher who agrees to help) and receive feedback on its value.

Keynote: To practise writing reports.

Parents are entitled to a lot of information about their child's progress

The parents of primary school leavers receive a report containing several pages of statistics, including all the information gained through the national assessments at Key Stages 1 and 2 in core subjects, together with (in many cases) a comment from a teacher or teachers on each subject: English, mathematics, science, history, geography, design and technology, information and communication technology, art, music and PE. Although parents will look at the statistical information, it is likely that they will be particularly interested in the nature of the teachers' comments, especially concerning their child's attitude, achievements, potential and non-academic strengths (see Figure 8). All the quantitative results from tests and tasks are expressed as levels on a common scale from 1 to 8; similarly, teacher assessments are placed within the same range of levels. Reports will also include a summary of school results for the year and national results from the previous year, allowing parents to compare broadly the progress of their children against others of the same age in the school and across the country. Not all parents realise that test results are only one measure of ability and that overall standards, particularly in very small schools, may vary considerably from year to year. Unfortunately, a great deal hinges on success in SATs, including parental perception of the quality of their children's education.

Keynote: To be familiar with parental entitlements.

All written comments will be interpreted by the parents

Teachers who write anything which is seen by parents have to make certain that they check the accuracy of its contents, the validity of its claims and the correctness of the syntax and spelling. Ambiguity in the way comments are phrased can create unnecessary alarm and, in extreme cases, anger from parents who may interpret your remarks as a personal affront. Head teachers are usually explicit about the kind of written information they wish to be included (if any), so teachers make every effort to conform to the agreed pattern. In addition to bland comments about progress, they try to include a positive remark about the

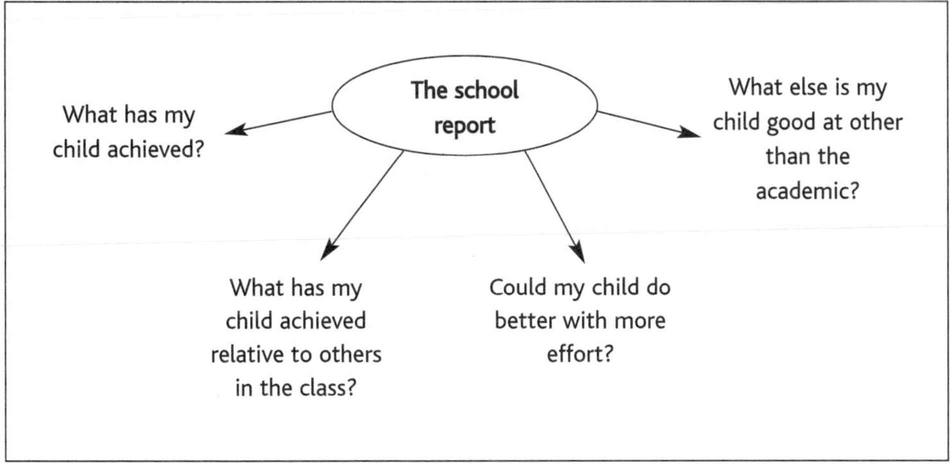

Figure 8 What parents want to know from school reports

child's attitude, contributions to the life of the class and school, and potential. While needing full information about their children's academic progress, parents of less able children, in particular, need to feel that there is hope for their offspring's future. This important truth should always be borne in mind when reporting.

Keynote: To write reports with the readers in mind.

Reports inform colleagues

Although a lot of information about pupils is transmitted to colleagues orally, the availability of a written record allows for a more considered view of progress and children's learning needs. In general, teachers are not concerned with a lot of fine detail but place great store by summarised comments for each child with regard to academic ability in core subjects, level of cooperation and behaviour, talents and skills, and enthusiasm for other curriculum areas. Some of this information can be expressed in numerical terms or grades; for example, a child may be working towards Level 3 in literacy and have achieved Level 2 in numeracy. However, the child's abilities may also be described rather than quantified; for example, in terms of handwriting neatness, confidence in the use of IT, engagement with historical themes, and level of contribution during collaborative endeavour. While it is true that new teachers soon discover these and similar forms of information for themselves, they are grateful for insights provided by the previous teacher to give them markers for planning and assessment. Straightforward and accessible records also help to inform substitute (supply) teachers who have to step in and take the class with little warning about ability groups and curriculum coverage.

Competence check

- ❑ I understand parents' entitlements concerning written information
- ❑ I know that both national assessments and teacher assessments are included in the report
- ❑ I have seen examples of completed reports and talked them through with an experienced colleague

CHAPTER 7

Critical Reflection (CR1)

The best teachers combine their talent, enthusiasm, hard work, personality and perseverance with a willingness to think about their teaching and make improvements on the basis of advice from others and intelligent reflection. In short, effective teachers never stop learning. This important quality is contained within a single specific statement but is implicit in many others:

CR1 To evaluate your own teaching critically and use this to improve your teaching effectiveness

What you need to take account of...

Critical evaluation is not the same as destructive criticism

A critical evaluation is achieved by scrutinising your practice openly and honestly, acknowledging strengths and weaknesses, and looking to ways of improving the situation. Constant fault-finding and criticism is not likely to enhance your teaching and is more likely to result in a downward spiralling of confidence. Your first question should always be, 'Where have I succeeded?' and not 'Where did I go wrong?'. Your mentor will often give you a helpful evaluation of a particular lesson, but you can self-evaluate at any time. By using Table 15 as a guide for your self-evaluation, you will probably find that most of the points can be graded as satisfactory or better.

Keynote: To look at achievements as well as shortcomings.

No lesson is perfect

Regardless of your skill in planning, awareness of individual needs, careful resourcing, excellent presentation, appropriate task-setting and perceptive assessments, every lesson can be improved. In truth, some lessons will be outstanding, some will be dire, and the majority are likely to be satisfactory. The secret is gradually to reduce the worst and increase the best. It is often difficult to know why some lessons 'take off' and others do not. There are sometimes factors beyond your immediate control that are affecting the situation (such as the fact that there is an after-school games match causing underlying excitement). Similarly, the presence or absence of one significant pupil can change the whole class atmosphere. Persevere to improve, learn from mistakes and press forward.

Keynote: To avoid too much self-analysis.

Table 15 Critical evaluation of progress in teaching

Rate yourself on a scale of Excellent (10)/Satisfactory (5)/Weak (1)

• Lesson preparation, including learning intentions	1..10
• Availability of resources	....
• Lesson introduction	....
• Explanation of tasks and activities	....
• Monitoring of pupil behaviour and application to task	....
• Assessment of pupils' progress	....
• Ending the lesson	....
• Links with other lessons	....
• Motivating pupils	....
• Self-motivation	....
• Use of other adults (see *FPT*, Chapter 4)	....
• Marking and homework procedures	....

Evaluations need to be focused

Although many teachers express satisfaction after what they perceive to have been a 'good' lesson or dismay following an 'awful' lesson, the criteria that they use to make such claims need to be more explicit, especially for student teachers. The most helpful evaluations relate to just one or two major aspects of the lesson (such as organisation or discipline) and the overall progress of the group or class (determined through written output, test results, pupils' comments, and so forth). Sometimes, a lesson seems to go smoothly for no reason other than the children are well occupied and get on with their work. On other occasions, an apparently disastrous type of lesson can seem less terrible if learning has taken place in spite of the turmoil. A lesson can be satisfactory in terms of the settled atmosphere, but poor in terms of the pupils' progress. By contrast, a lesson in which there appears to be an excessive amount of disruptive behaviour may have much firmer learning outcomes. Close analysis of lesson components is useful but does not give a complete picture as many elements of lesson management and organisation are closely related; failure in one area (especially preparation and class control) can result in disappointment, regardless of the effort put into others.

Keynote: To pinpoint key areas for close analysis.

Evaluations also need to take a long-term view

Your lesson may have lacked the quality and precision that you would have ideally liked, but you may have made substantial progress in building your confidence, working with other teachers, grouping children imaginatively or coping with a difficult child. Your immediate evaluation may find a number of areas for improvement, yet your long-term prospects for effective teaching may have been improved due to your willingness to tackle demanding elements of classroom life. The impact of your teaching has to be viewed as a whole, as some days will go better than others; it is the overall improvement across a period of time that counts. The fable about a race between a hare and tortoise may not be wholly applicable to work in school, but steady, consistent application to the job pays dividends.

Keynote: To measure progress over both the short and long term.

Meeting the standards must espouse creative teaching

Despite its formal tone and fixed requirements, Circular 02/02 (TTA 2002a) stresses that professionalism is more than meeting a set of discrete standards. It requires an individual teacher's creativity, commitment, enthusiasm, intellect and management skills. When you evaluate your teaching, you need to bear in mind the extent to which your teaching conforms with these qualities as well as the planning, delivery and assessment cycle. It is important not to be overwhelmed by the many demands that meeting the standards makes and neglect your own instinct and spontaneity. As an intelligent and thinking person, you will need to be familiar with the vocabulary of teaching and discuss different aspects of your work as a teacher with colleagues and fellow students. In this way you will be both a teacher of children and an adult learner. However your creativity will be stifled if you passively accept what others say about teaching without establishing your own educational values and priorities.

Despite the efforts of education policy-makers to impose different curriculum and systems of teaching on teachers, your success as a practitioner ultimately depends on five things:

1. Your appetite for the job.
2. Your willingness to learn from your mistakes.

3. Your passion for seeing children learn.
4. Your integrity and educational ideals.
5. Your personality and ability to relate to colleagues and children.

With these points in mind, it is encouraging that the opening section of the latest set of standards for QTS commence with 'Professional Values and Practice' (see also Cole 2002). In Part II of this book these standards will be used as the basis for an exploration of the way in which you can successfully meet the requirements without losing sight of your educational principles.

Keynote: To adopt a positive and thoughtful approach to teaching.

Competence check

- ❑ I am spending time thinking about why I do things as well as how I do them
- ❑ I am using a structured approach in my evaluations
- ❑ I am using my evaluations and reflections to enhance my own learning

PART II

Standards for Qualified Teacher Status

Trainee teachers ('Trainees') who are to be awarded Qualified Teacher Status (QTS) must understand and uphold the professional code of the General Teaching Council for England by demonstrating competence across the requirements listed below. The detailed comment contained in Part II conforms closely to the information provided in the *Handbook of Guidance on QTS Standards and ITT Requirements* (TTA 2002b), and the numbering system found in the Handbook is indicated in brackets. Only statements relevant to the primary phase are included and in some cases the original wording has been slightly modified for ease of use. Each statement is accompanied by three additional sets of information intended to give you an indication of the sorts of skills, experience and attitudes that should characterise your planning, teaching and class management:

- *Implications for classroom practice*... giving an 'at-a-glance' summary of key points;
- *Indicative forms of evidence*... providing a straightforward check list to indicate whether the standard has been achieved;
- *Specific forms of evidence*... offering an 'ideal' description of each indicative element.

When considering the statements, it is important to understand that evidence should not be confused with 'proof'. Proof is absolute and undeniable and does not have a role to play in assessing competence level, while evidence is in the form of *indicators* for each standard, open to professional judgement and interpretation, and necessary in evaluating your progress. The information contained in the remainder of this book will help you to make sense of the available evidence about effective classroom practice, which is normally discerned in one or more of four ways:

1. Feedback from a teacher or tutor observing a lesson.

2. Evaluative comments you have written in a log or commentary.
3. Discussions about issues with a teacher or tutor in which you demonstrate your understanding by what you say.
4. Information found in your teaching file, especially lesson plan details and assessment records.

It is not possible or desirable to provide individual pieces of evidence for every detail of every standard, so some aggregating is inevitable. For instance, if the lesson tasks are suitably differentiated then you will be taking account of individual differences too. Similarly, managing pupil behaviour successfully invariably means that you have established a good working relationship with the children. Links between standards are made explicit in the Handbook of Guidance and some have been combined in the descriptions that form the major component of Part II.

The majority of evidence about competence in a particular area of expertise will be gained during work placements, but some have to be demonstrated in other ways. For instance, some teacher training is located in areas of the country where there is little cultural or language variation. In such cases, exposure to the issues may have to be gained through the use of video, contact with those who have experienced such working situations or case study examples. Again, not every trainee has opportunity to take part in a formally organised parent consultation event to report on pupil progress. In such cases, a mock interview may have to be set up using (say) a teaching assistant as a substitute 'parent'. Sometimes it will be necessary to give a verbal explanation to a tutor or school mentor about your grasp of a school-related issue; for instance, about your knowledge of the Code of Practice. These examples serve to underline the point that a demonstration of competence is not always straightforward and evidence of competence is not solely found in classroom practice.

IMPORTANT NOTE

The descriptions attached to the competence checks are intended for your *own* use and not as a mechanical 'tick list' for assessment purposes. They do, however, provide a starting point for evaluating progress and an agenda for discussions with class teachers, mentors and tutors.

If you are in the *early* stages of training, you will still be 'working towards' most of the ideal descriptions of suitable evidence attached to the standard statements. Even if you are approaching the *end* of training, you should still be cautious about trying to apply the criteria rigidly to individual sessions, as the perfect lesson and ideal trainee teacher is a rarity. On some days you may feel that your performance falls below what you had hoped for, but this is a common experience and should not be a source of depression. All teachers have ups and downs, so an evaluation of competence is best carried out when you have taught for a length of time and can review a *series* of lessons and a range of classroom experience. It is important to take a balanced view of your progress over time and not to imagine that one poor lesson spells the end of your teaching career!

As with all learning, it is important to gain advice from more experienced colleagues in school. Although your instinct will often provide a useful guide as to how well a lesson or a series of lessons went, an informed opinion from the class teacher, mentor, tutor or a fellow-student will help you to achieve a more balanced perspective. You should view their comments and feedback as a means of helping you to become a more effective teacher.

The following guidelines are largely based on two of the sub-sections found in the Handbook of Guidance, namely, 'Professional Values and Practice' (sub-section 1) and 'Teaching' (sub-section 3). The descriptions do not refer specifically to standards found in sub-section 2, 'Knowledge and Understanding', though a number of them are subsumed within other standard requirements; for example, standard S2.7 'Promoting Good Behaviour' is incorporated into S3.3.9. The effective use of ICT (S2.5) and information about the new Code of Practice (S2.6) are explored in Part I of the book. A number of the standards have been merged and standard number S3.3.2 has not been included as it deals with curriculum coverage. For full details of all the standards and the precise wording used, refer to the Handbook. After each set of descriptions there is either a summary *comment* and/or a *case study* to offer insights into the way that trainee teachers have confronted some of the issues that relate to the standard. Although the accounts (including all names used) are fictional, they are based on genuine situations and people.

CHAPTER 8

Professional Values and Practice

Standard

Trainees should have high expectations of all pupils, respect their social, cultural, linguistic, religious and ethnic backgrounds and be committed to raising their educational achievement (S1.1).

Trainees should treat pupils consistently, with respect and consideration and show a concern for their development as learners (S1.2).

Implications for practice

1. Expectations are based on the child's potential and capacity to learn.
2. All children are given the opportunity to contribute to lessons without fear or favour.
3. All children are encouraged to achieve to the limit of their intellectual capacity.
4. Account is taken of the fact that children learn in different ways.

Indicative forms of evidence

1. The children respond positively to lessons because they are relevant and interesting.
2. An appropriate amount of time and attention for particular children is provided during lessons and a similar amount of encouragement is offered for each child.
3. Expectations of high standards of work are established and children are offered appropriate support to achieve them.
4. A variety of teaching and learning strategies are used to inspire and involve the children, including didactic teaching, collaborative group work, question-and-answer sessions, and practical tasks.

Specific forms of evidence

Children's responses to your lessons...

Children are consistently enthusiastic and disappointed when the lesson ends. They work well and do their best to achieve high standards and please you. Their questions and comments indicate that they have not only grasped the basic content of the lesson but are thinking for themselves and eager to extend their knowledge.

Provision of time and enthusiasm...

You are proactive in attending to children's specific needs and respond positively to requests for assistance. You do your best to allocate time fairly among the children and show an equal level of commitment to all of them.

Support to achieve high standards of work...

You demonstrate a willingness to explain carefully what is required and provide them with strategies to complete their work, monitor progress closely and offer either suggestions (to encourage self-reliance) or specific guidance about improvement (to scaffold learning more tightly). You designate tasks and activities that are appropriate to the children's learning needs, give constructive feedback and praise true endeavour.

Using a variety of teaching and learning strategies...

You incorporate a range of direct and indirect teaching and learning into lessons with reference to previous assessments of children's needs and ongoing monitoring of their progress. You adjust your explanations and teaching methods for different children whenever possible, using illustrations, analogies, stories and visual aids to allow them to grasp concepts, understand techniques and develop skills. You allow time for questions and actively encourage children to try things for themselves, being sure to commend genuine effort and celebrate small achievements.

Comment

Every teacher strives to secure a positive relationship with children as soon as possible and to be consistent in approach. While it is important to give all children a fair proportion of your time, it is frequently the case that during a particular lesson certain children will demand more attention than others do. However, this time imbalance can be addressed by ensuring that the children who received relatively little attention are compensated in subsequent sessions. Consequently, over a longer period, all children should receive a similar proportion of your time. You will need to take account of a minority of children who make it clear that they prefer to be left alone to get on with their work as far as possible. At the other extreme, some vulnerable children make constant demands on any adult willing to offer them assistance. In these situations, you have to evaluate the extent to which you should offer immediate support and how much you should encourage the children to try things for themselves. Every teacher wants the children to be successful, so you should transmit these aspirations to them clearly. If you don't tell them you care, they won't know!

Case study

Tina was teaching in an inner-city school where there were many varied cultures represented. She was passionate about giving all children an equal and fair chance so, while being careful not to patronise them, Tina made it her aim to speak to each child individually for at least a minute every day. After a week of teaching them, she realised that maintaining the practice was far harder than she had thought, so to help fulfil her aim she took to standing outside the classroom door at the start of the day, shaking each child's hand and greeting them one at a time. Although some of the children (and Tina herself) initially found this embarrassing, it quickly became a valued part of the routine. On one occasion that Tina was a little late reaching the classroom in the morning, the children were waiting outside in the corridor, reluctant to enter before receiving their 'Big Hello' as Tina called it. Later in the placement, Tina gradually learned to greet children in their first language, a practice that pleased parents and was the catalyst for an assembly presentation on the theme of 'One Family'.

Standard

Trainees demonstrate and promote the positive values, attitudes and behaviour that they expect from their pupils (S1.3).

Implications for practice

1. Cooperation is emphasised and applauded.
2. Genuine effort is praised.
3. Composure is maintained, even under duress.
4. Value judgements are suspended until a situation has been clarified.

Indicative forms of evidence

1. There is more approving comment rather than criticism, so that children feel that they are valued and their opinions respected.
2. A lot of encouragement is provided during lessons and when children have completed tasks.

3. Voice tone is strong when required but a level tone is employed to promote and maintain a calm atmosphere.
4. Children are invited to give explanations about their actions before decisions are reached about who was in the wrong.

Specific forms of evidence

Approval rather than criticism...

Your comments are largely positive in tone and you always try to find something to approve before making criticisms. The children are happy to establish eye contact with you when you speak to them, indicating trust and confidence in your judgement.

Encouragement and praise...

Your encouragement is specific and engenders a fresh determination in children to persevere. You praise sincere effort and help children to maintain a sense of purpose, even when they are struggling.

Using a level tone...

You maintain a high level of self-control when addressing children and show a command of the situation without needing to hector or bully them. You can speak strongly when necessary without becoming overwrought or irritable.

Asking for explanations...

You positively promote the opportunity for children to justify their actions before making a calm evaluation of the position rather than jumping to hasty conclusions. You listen carefully while children speak and allow them to defend their actions. You arbitrate fairly and explain the reasons for your decisions to them.

Comment

Teachers are role models for children, whether they like it or not. Your behaviour will not only affect the learning climate but also influence the way that the children relate to others, both inside and outside the classroom. Trainee teachers may be surprised at the number of times that children justify their actions at home by claiming that *Miss Brown says it's alright.* Parents get used to hearing the names of favourite teachers being used by their children, and expect that the influence they exert will be positive. It is worth carrying out an 'attitude check' on yourself in school to ensure that your body language, tone of voice and responses to pupils and colleagues are characterised by vibrancy and infectious enthusiasm. This approach does not, of course, involve the use of exaggerated gesture and unnatural bonhomie, but rather a determination to be the sort of person with whom others feel comfortable.

Case study

Dishi had always wanted to be a teacher and was very excited about her school experience in a village school quite close to a large town. She was quite disappointed, therefore, when she found that her class of eight- and nine-year-olds had little appetite for learning and seemed reluctant to try out anything that required them to be adventurous. After a time, Dishi discerned that the children's tentativeness was rooted in their fear of failure. After discussion with the class teacher and mentor, she implemented what she referred to as her 'One for all and all for one' approach, in which there were four simple rules:

1. No-one is criticised for trying.
2. Everyone has a right to be wrong sometimes.
3. When one person succeeds, we all succeed.
4. Speak as we would be spoken to.

Although Dishi's approach was sorely tested at times and some children seemed reluctant to cooperate fully, by the end of her placement there was a much bolder and more creative learning climate. There was agreement that Dishi's positive approach had made a difference to the children's enthusiasm for learning, willingness to face new challenges and appetite to grapple with unfamiliar or unpromising situations.

Standard

Trainees can communicate sensitively and effectively with parents and carers as partners in learning, recognising their roles in pupils' learning, and their rights, responsibilities and interests in this (S1.4).

Implications for practice

1. Interaction with parents and carers happens regularly.
2. Opportunities are found to inform parents about the curriculum and their children's progress.
3. Opportunity is created for parents to be involved in homework tasks.
4. Parents are spoken to courteously and their questions are answered openly.

Indicative forms of evidence

1. Making an effort to meet parents informally at the start and end of the day.
2. Discussing samples of children's work with their parents.

3. Encouraging the children to consult adults at home about homework.
4. Treating parents impartially and making a serious effort to respond to their concerns when they raise them.

Specific forms of evidence

Meeting parents informally...

You ensure that you are sufficiently well organised to be available at key times for parents and initiate conversations in a relaxed but purposeful way. You show an interest in what parents say to you, offer positive comment about classroom life, answer their questions sincerely and respond politely, even on occasions when you feel that the parent is being unreasonable.

Discussing samples of children's work...

You are familiar with individual children's work and progress, and can speak with authority about what they have accomplished using vocabulary that is suitable for a lay person. You explain clearly and unambiguously, avoiding specialist education terms and being careful not to come across as supercilious.

Adult involvement in homework...

You set homework tasks that invite adult participation but are not dependent upon it. You encourage the children to ask parents for assistance if required and explain what form it might take.

Treating parents seriously...

You make parents feel significant and welcome by speaking in a natural and friendly manner, but not patronising them. You take account of their views and make it clear from your responses that you take their comments seriously and consider them when making future decisions.

Comment

All parents are interested in their children's education and welfare, and the vast majority are delighted when given specific opportunities to contribute. There is, however, a need to be careful not to give the impression that parents are doing the teachers' work for them. There is a difference between, on the one hand, affording parents and carers their rights as guardians by volunteering information about the children and, on the other hand, overwhelming them with unnecessary details about their children's progress or placing unreasonable demands on their time. Involvement of parents is essential, but it is vexatious for them if it seems to them that teachers are reneging on their responsibilities. A good example of this tension is hearing children read aloud. In the past, teachers of younger pupils spent a lot of their time hearing readers on a one-to-one basis. This responsibility has now largely passed to teaching assistants and parents. If, however, a parent consistently hears her child read, and then becomes aware that the teacher hardly ever does so, it can cause confusion or resentment. As the trainee teacher you have to conform to the existing school practice, but it is worth being sensitive to the issues associated with parental involvement and striving to make them feel included without taking them for granted.

Case study

Emma was teaching a challenging Year 6 class in a depressed area of the country where parental involvement in school was adversely affected by social conditions. She found that children were not always completing their maths homework and they produced a variety of excuses about what had happened. With the head teacher's and class teacher's approval, Emma sent a polite note home to parents explaining the difficulties that a failure to complete homework created and requesting help, but the problem persisted. Emma decided that a different approach was needed so, with the encouragement and assistance of the teacher, she told the class that any parent who wanted to do so could have a photograph of themselves on the school website. To everyone's surprise, the idea was a success and within two weeks nearly half of the parents had come into school to have their photograph taken with the digital camera. The children who were in a position to do so sent the photographs to their home computers. Every parent who had been photographed was given a colour printout. Several of the parents sent pictures of their families via the Internet to the school. By the time Emma completed her placement, every parent in the class had responded and, after a suggestion from one mum that it would be fun to allow parents to dress up if they wanted to do so, some parents wore traditional costumes for their photographs. Best of all, the relationship between school staff and parents improved and even maths homework began to appear more regularly! After Emma had left the school, the head teacher designated a large notice board for the purpose of displaying interesting and celebratory photographs of parents and their children.

Standard

Trainees can contribute to, and share responsibly in, the corporate life of schools or other relevant settings (S1.5).

Implications for practice

1. Contributing as a junior member of the staff team.
2. Showing a high level of mature responsibility.

3. Showing a willingness to contribute skills and knowledge to the corporate enterprise.
4. Demonstrating trustworthiness and reliability.

Indicative forms of evidence

1. Endeavouring to become a team member, showing a keenness to learn, improve understanding and contribute ideas.
2. Behaving like a novice teacher rather than a member of the support staff.
3. Volunteering to do tasks rather than waiting to be asked.
4. Making every possible effort to make a success of tasks by working hard, taking advice and persevering to completion.

Specific forms of evidence

Junior member of staff...

You successfully model yourself on the highest professional standards exhibited by colleagues, in speech, action and attitude. You are careful not to give the impression of knowing more than you do, but volunteer suggestions and insights as appropriate. You listen carefully to advice and, by commenting constructively, show that you intend to act upon it.

Behaving as a novice teacher...

Your ability to organise and manage the class, and your attitude in out-of-class settings compares favourably with many trainee teachers. You do not attempt to ingratiate yourself with the children but enjoy a strong adult–child relationship with them. You show adeptness in organising and managing teaching, and dependability in out-of-class settings.

Volunteering your skills...

You offer your time and expertise in extra-curricular activities (including educational visits) and school events by liaising closely with colleagues. You are generous in sharing any abilities you possess but careful not to allow additional commitments to detract from the regular business of planning, teaching and assessing work.

Striving hard to succeed...

You demonstrate a keen desire to develop and enhance your professional expertise by adopting an industrious approach to the work and learning from good practice. You maintain a record of key points and issues for consideration and use them in evaluating your progress.

Comment

The transition from outsider to insider is never easy to achieve within the few weeks that you are on school placement. Nevertheless, it is surprising how quickly most teachers will accept and value your contribution if you display a wholehearted approach to your work, evidenced through conscientious planning, open dialogue with staff and a willingness to learn and contribute. Even if you sometimes feel that you are being kept on the margins of school life because of your student status, perseverance and a positive outlook can transform the situation. Teachers are always thankful for a trainee who is genuinely enthusiastic, shows a capacity for hard work and learns from mistakes.

Case study

Ben had struggled with his teaching from the day he arrived at the new school placement and, despite having succeeded in previous school experiences, simply could not settle or make smooth progress. It was difficult to pinpoint the problem, as Ben planned carefully, enjoyed working with the children and got on reasonably well with the class teacher, but something seemed to 'block' the way. Ben's progress was adequate to achieve success but he knew that he was under-performing and felt quite demoralised as a result. The breakthrough came when the annual 'June Fayre' was held just after the summer half term. Ben had gained experience in organising events before he commenced his teacher training and was quickly making a thoughtful contribution during staff discussions. The head teacher noticed his obvious enthusiasm and expertise, and asked if he would help to organise the entertainment, which Ben was pleased to do. He proved to be adept at the task and even managed to persuade a local professional footballer to make a guest appearance and sign autographs. Ben worked with the music specialist and organised a group of children to perform some songs and poetry. He also charmed a few teachers into singing a comic song (to great applause!). To complete a memorable day, Ben used his skills as a DJ and was credited with helping to make the event one of the most successful ever. More significantly for Ben was the fact that during the preparation for the day and beyond, his status in the school rose considerably and his relationship with the children was transformed. Everything began to fall into place and Ben not only finished the placement strongly, but also applied for, and was appointed as an NQT in the school.

Standard

Trainees understand the contribution that support staff and other professionals make to teaching and learning (S1.6).

Trainees work collaboratively with specialist trainees and other colleagues and, with the help of an experienced teacher as appropriate, manage the work of teaching assistants or other adults to enhance pupils' learning (S3.3.13).

Implications for practice

1. Making best use of adult expertise.
2. Respecting the views and opinions of support staff.
3. Showing awareness of the role played by professionals from outside the school.
4. Showing awareness of the role of specialist staff in other educational settings.

Indicative forms of evidence

1. Lesson plans specify the part played by each adult.
2. Support staff are actively involved in decisions.
3. The role and potential contribution of outside agencies is clarified and understood.
4. Involvement with planning for trips and/or educational visits.

Specific forms of evidence

Lesson plans...

You describe each adult's role clearly in your lesson plans, identify goals for each activity group and provide assessment criteria from which the adults are able to make an evaluation of the children's progress.

Consulting other adults...

You discuss with support staff the plans that you have made that impact upon their work and describe their role and your expectations for children's learning during the lesson or lessons. You invite and listen to their suggestions and incorporate them wherever appropriate, explaining your decisions for doing so to them.

Role of outside agencies...

You engage in a well-informed discussion with a knowledgeable staff member and gain first-hand experience by working alongside an experienced colleague. You are able to speak with some knowledge about outside agencies, their broad responsibilities and when they might become involved in school affairs. You are familiar with school procedures for involving an agency.

Involvement in school visits...

You help to plan a visit with a qualified member of staff and liaise with the specialist at the visit site, demonstrating an awareness of the role that the site specialist might play and using the information provided to develop schemes of work, follow-up materials and records of the visit (such as a photo montage).

Comment

It is difficult for student teachers to plan lessons that take account of their own role and the activities that children will undertake, while also having regard for the role and responsibilities of the other adults involved. However, the significance of support staff is increasing and their contribution often involves responsibility for a group of children and may even include some time spent in charge of the whole class. Consequently, they must be treated as colleagues. Supporting adults are referred to by a variety of titles and this is reflected both in the work they do and the amount they are paid. A 'classroom assistant' is a general helper, who deals with practical issues such as organising consumables and photocopying resources. A 'learning support assistant' is appointed to help a child or children with special educational needs and will, as a result, have a more narrowly defined role. A 'teaching assistant' is often someone who has a range of well-developed skills and may have undergone extensive training (DfEE 2000b). Teaching assistants (or their equivalent) are able to supervise and teach small numbers of children and provide specific expertise in, for example, use of computer software. It is important to be aware of the limitations and capabilities of support staff, especially when you are planning for the whole class. As the other adults may be older and more experienced than you, it is essential to gain their confidence, admit that you are willing to learn and treat them with the utmost courtesy, while at the same time being clear about what you are hoping they can achieve. Support staff appreciate being asked two questions from time to time:

- Are you happy with what you are being expected to do?
- Is there anything that you would like me to say or do that would help you with your job?

The use of support staff is particularly important during educational visits and outdoor activities, when everyone's role is made explicit. In any situation where there is an element of risk, the organiser (usually the class teacher) will have made sure that nothing is left to chance, but you should take every opportunity to be involved with the planning, preparation and management. Remember that next time *you* may be the one who has to take the main responsibility for organising – when you have your own class! (See also section 3.1.5.)

Standard

Trainees are able to improve their own teaching, by evaluating it, learning from the effective practice of others and from evidence. They are motivated and able to take increasing responsibility for their own professional development (S1.7).

Implications for practice

1. Reflecting on the effectiveness of classroom practice.
2. Regularly observing other teachers at work and taking note of their lesson strategies.
3. Keeping abreast of research evidence and opinion to evaluate its potential impact on practice.
4. Systematically monitoring professional development as a means of enhancing effectiveness.

Indicative forms of evidence

1. Ability to analyse classroom practice effectively, both verbally and on paper, identify the values that underpin actions and the impact upon children's learning.
2. Ability to use evidence gleaned from a range of teaching to inform your own practice.
3. Ability to evaluate research findings and a variety of opinions in the light of classroom experience.
4. Ability to set realistic and appropriate goals and targets for professional improvement.

Specific forms of evidence

Analysing practice...

You take a decisive but realistic view of your strengths and weaknesses, consider advice carefully and devise strategies with targets to remedy or improve your practice. You regularly log key issues and critical events that you have noted, together with your own reflections about their classroom implications.

Using evidence to inform practice...

You systematically observe general and pre-determined aspects of more experienced teachers' work, consider the relevance of their practice for your own development as a teacher, and modify your teaching approach accordingly.

Evaluating research findings...

You gain information from a variety of reliable sources and evaluate them in the light of your experience and advice from experienced colleagues. Subsequently, you discuss the claims with a teacher or tutor, or make a concise written summary about their implications for classroom practice in the light of your present understanding and aspirations for increased effectiveness as a teacher.

Setting realistic targets...

You use information from your lesson evaluations to identify key aspects of classroom practice and subject knowledge that need strengthening. You discuss your progress fully with tutors, devise sensible targets within a given time frame, and formulate strategies to attain them. You then monitor your progress using evidence from observers' feedback, children's responses and your own deliberations.

Comment

It is important to regularly evaluate your classroom practice, reflect carefully on its effectiveness and gain support from others on ways to improve. However, it is inadvisable to concentrate purely on the less developed features of your teaching and marginalise the stronger points. Too much effort expended on your shortcomings will be counterproductive if it results in a neglect of the areas in which you feel more confident. For example, you may find direct 'stand and deliver' teaching with intensive teacher–pupil interaction more difficult than organising group work, monitoring progress and providing formative assessment (see Clarke 2001). While it would be legitimate to explore ways of enhancing your direct teaching, it would be foolish to assume that there was no room for improvement in the way you handle group activities. Furthermore, it is perfectly reasonable to enhance your teaching strengths if they aid children's learning and help you to feel more confident. Improved practice does not come about merely by asking experienced colleagues for 'tips', but understanding their reasons for using certain strategies and discerning whether you are yet in a position to emulate people of their experience. Consequently, the incorporation of other teachers' methods or of research findings into your teaching should not be done unthinkingly, but only after very careful consideration. Some techniques have to be stored away and 'banked' for a future day when you are qualified, have your own class and feel better able to explore different approaches while not under constant scrutiny.

Case study

Beth felt that she was progressing well on school placement until the head teacher decided to observe all the student teachers as part of his quality assurance monitoring. Beth was nervous but not unduly anxious as she had been commended as a conscientious teacher by both of her previous mentors and felt at ease with the Year 4 class she was teaching. The lesson ran smoothly and the children responded well to her prompting. Beth waited with a glow of anticipation for the head's approval after the lesson ended but to her surprise and alarm she did not receive the glowing accolade that she was expecting. The head thanked her for the careful way she had organised the lesson and the thoroughness of her planning; he also praised her for the way that she had dealt firmly with a couple of excitable boys and her positive manner. However, he alerted her to a number of issues that she needed to consider in more depth, notably the highly predictable way that she went about her teaching and her failure to take advantage of the children's curiosity. He told her that she had mastered the rudiments of the job and would, at this rate, become quite a good teacher. If she wanted to be 'better than average', she would need to be more creative and imaginative in the way she presented the lesson's content and tasks. He explained that although children need a structure, they flourish with teachers who can inject a touch of unpredictability into lessons and fully 'milk' every learning opportunity. Beth thanked the head but was inwardly seething about his comments. That evening, she discussed the matter with her friend, Faye, and they agreed that the head was out of touch with the realities of teaching. Over the next few days, however, Beth slowly came to realise that although her systematic approach was praiseworthy, she was tending to view the process of learning from her own perspective rather than that of the child. Although she continued to feel slightly aggrieved at the head's assessment of her teaching, it alerted her to the fact that professional development is an ongoing challenge for every teacher. By the time she completed her placement, Beth was pleased when the mentor noted that she was not only a conscientious trainee who applied herself to her work but was also keen to develop and improve her creativity and exploit every learning opportunity. Beth understood better what her tutor had once said about the best teachers being the most willing to learn. Perhaps the head teacher wasn't so far wrong after all!

Standard

Trainees are aware of, and work within, the statutory frameworks relating to teachers' responsibilities (S1.8).

Implications for practice

1. Keen awareness of child protection issues.
2. Familiarity with procedures for children who have special educational needs.
3. Adopting a responsible attitude towards children's safety in school and during visits.
4. Awareness of the need to maintain a professional approach in school.

Indicative forms of evidence

1. Sensitivity towards the potential physical hazards and emotional vulnerability of children.

2. Inclusion of children with differing needs through appropriate planning, classroom management, interaction, time during lessons and allocation of tasks.
3. Forward thinking, planning and risk assessment to avoid exposure to harm, ensure the appropriateness and safety of activities and monitor children's movements.
4. Responsible behaviour and action in school.

Specific forms of evidence

Sensitivity towards hazards...

You carry out a risk assessment prior to activities, seek advice in advance of large space lessons (such as PE, swimming), offer clear and unambiguous guidance about safety factors and procedures, and take particular care with vulnerable children. You take account of these potential hazards during the lesson by giving careful instructions to the children and maintaining firm control to minimise the likelihood of injury.

Inclusion of children...

You show through your words and actions that you value the unique contribution of each child, and make every effort to ensure that lessons motivate and facilitate achievement and fulfilment at the highest possible level. This is reflected in the amount of attention that you give to each child and the way that as far as possible you accommodate the differing learning needs of children, including those for whom English is an additional language.

Risk assessment...

You evaluate the risk of each activity on the basis of the school's health and safety guidelines, advice from experienced colleagues and mentors, and your professional judgement about potential hazards. The assessment is noted in your lesson plan and influences your actions to safeguard pupils' security during the lesson.

Acting responsibly in school...

You are polite to all staff and children, adopt a personable and enthusiastic approach to your work, listen carefully to others, make every effort to conform to school priorities without compromising your integrity, and use your abilities to the full. You show decorum at all times, respond positively to school life, and have an affirming attitude in the things you say and do.

Comment

Health and safety in school is referred to in NC2000 (DfEE/QCA 1999) and applies to science, DT, ICT, art & design, and PE. When working with tools, equipment and materials in practical activities and different environments, including unfamiliar ones, children should be taught:

- about hazards, risks and risk control
- to assess risks and take steps to control them
- to use information to assess risk
- to manage the environment safely
- to explain the steps they take to control risks.

CHAPTER 9

Teaching

Introduction

It is perfectly possible for children to learn without being taught, but they generally make much better progress when there is a more knowledgeable and experienced adult available to guide them through the complex processes involved. The clearer you are about what you are trying to achieve with the children and what you hope they will learn, the easier it is to formulate a teaching plan and approach to achieve these objectives. However, the best laid plans and most sophisticated teaching strategies available count for little unless you have taken careful account of the children's existing knowledge, understanding and motivation. Even if you technically meet the considerable number of standards listed below, your teaching will lack power and effectiveness unless you can translate lesson plans into creative teaching. In doing so you will need to draw on your enthusiasm, verve and imagination so that the children capture the same sense of urgency and excitement that shines out of you.

Planning, expectations and targets

Standard

Trainees set challenging teaching and learning objectives which are relevant to all pupils in their classes, based on a knowledge of:

- *the pupils*
- *evidence of their past and current achievement*
- *the expected standards for pupils of the relevant age range*
- *the range and content of work relevant to pupils in that age range (S3.1.1).*

Implications for practice

1. Teaching and learning objectives are considered together.
2. Children learn best in a variety of ways.
3. Previous attainment and achievements have to be taken into account when planning lessons.
4. Maturity rate and experience of the children are factors to consider when setting appropriate work and activities.

Indicative forms of evidence

1. Teaching strategies and approach are modified, depending on what children should be learning.
2. Allowance is made for children who learn at different speeds, require less or more adult support, and benefit from learning aids.
3. The type of work set and the expectations of what children can achieve builds on previous attainment and sets targets that are realistic yet stretching.
4. The vocabulary used, level of peer support offered and concentration span is appropriate for the children's age and maturity.

Specific forms of evidence

Teaching strategies and approach...

Your planning takes account of the occasions when it is appropriate for children to be given information directly (e.g. providing factual content), when they need to investigate things for themselves (e.g. directed play), when it is best to work on their own (e.g. imaginative writing) and when collaboration is preferable (e.g. science problem solving). You ensure that visual aids and stimuli are available to support and enhance learning when conceptual understanding requires concrete support.

Allowance for different children...

Your planning provides that at each lesson stage the vocabulary, questions, concepts, activities and adult support allow all children to engage with learning, find fulfilment in the work and attain their potential. You are therefore sensitive to what you say, how you say it and when you say it. For example, you give slower thinkers more time to respond to questions, offer plenty of encouragement to under-confident children and set challenges for the more able. Careful observation of pupil progress is made and shared with the children during the lesson (Harding and Meldon-Smith 2000).

Expectations and targets…

Your expectations are clarified in advance of the lesson through discussion with teachers and examination of pupils' previous achievements, explained clearly to children at the start and attainable through their concentrated effort. Specific learning targets are talked through with the children, and identified and monitored during the lesson. Assessment of progress is manageable, closely related to lesson intentions and, over the longer term, carried out with reference to national expectations (e.g. NC levels).

Account taken of age and maturity…

Your planning ensures that less productive and slower workers are motivated to achieve success by involving them in tasks that lie within their capability, yet offer some challenge. Open-ended extension activities are provided for faster and more productive children to achieve success. Your planning also allows for the fact that some children apply themselves to tasks better than others by building in some flexibility to the lesson. For example, you may allow a normally unsettled child who is engrossed in an activity to continue to do so despite the fact that others have moved on to something different.

Comment

It is useful to distinguish between *planning* and *plans*. Planning is the process by which a plan is formulated. Plans that are created by others cannot be 'taken off the shelf' and opened like a can of beans! They should be the end product of a considerable amount of thought with regard to the required curriculum, the learning needs of children, the availability of resources and (sometimes) the physical constraints of particular classroom situations. The best-written plans result from a synthesis of detailed and in-depth thinking. They contain sufficient information to ensure that the lesson flows smoothly but are written concisely so that, in the pressure of a lesson, they are accessible and useable. In planning, a careful consideration about the use of aids and resource material is very important in three ways: (a) so that they enhance the teaching; (b) so that learning is made more straightforward; (c) so that all children benefit from using them. While it is imperative that activities and tasks are differentiated in such a way that all children engage with appropriate lesson material, it is also essential to take close account of the organisational implications of providing a range of activities for children of differing abilities and aptitude. Finally, all planning requires attention to the things that children have previously experienced and learned, as well as their potential for further achievement. In practice, this means information gleaned from the class teacher and, perhaps, familiarity with children's previous test results or early years' profiles, allow you to make informed decisions. Over time, and as you get to know the children better, you will become more secure about evaluating their ability and potential, so that you increasingly become the guardian of assessment information rather than an onlooker.

Case study

Sue was pleased when a friend told her about a publication that contained a series of lesson plans for science that were easy to use. As Sue had always struggled with the subject, she was delighted to have additional resources and support for her teaching. She came across a lesson suggestion for promoting scientific enquiry using simple resources such as paper of differing thickness, adhesive tape and paper clips. The activity involved producing a stable structure, no more than a hand's size that would rotate and stay in the air for five seconds when dropped from heights varying between one and two metres. Sue knew instinctively that her class of ten- and eleven-year-olds would find the investigation both stimulating and worthwhile and, for the first time ever, she looked forward to the lesson. As well as the simplicity of resources, Sue was relieved to be able to use the lesson plan more or less as published. Things began promisingly. After an introduction in which she talked to the children about the concepts underpinning flight and how objects heavier than air stayed aloft, Sue then explained carefully what the children were being asked to do. The resources for the lesson were neatly stacked on a table and she had reproduced a prediction and results sheet direct from the book of ideas. Unfortunately, Sue's faith in the lesson plan was soon shaken. First, a child asked whether they had to work in pairs or alone; in all her excitement about the lesson, Sue had completely overlooked this elementary point. Then another child asked if they could use scissors. Again, Sue realised that she had failed to read the plan carefully and had not even thought about having a sufficient supply of scissors. Once these matters had been sorted out, Sue reminded them to make some predictions about which paper was best suited for flight and the smallest number of paper clips that could be used to keep the craft upright. Such was their enthusiasm to get on with the practical activity, however, the children gave little serious thought to this part of the work and they launched into the main task with great gusto. A number of problems emerged, not least the fact that some children began hoarding materials when it became clear that there would be a shortage of paper clips. The reels of tape were messy to cut up, so Sue found herself spending a lot of time helping with this task. Many of the children could not hold the craft at a height of two metres, so began standing on chairs. The tape ran out before several groups could complete their experiments, leading to complaints and cries of dissatisfaction. Sue just about coped with the demands made of her and placated the disappointed children by promising to find time to let them complete their work later in the day. Storing the items used during the session and clearing up afterwards were also challenges to her management skills and patience. Sue felt drained of energy by the end but she was also a lot wiser. She realised that the mere provision of a lesson plan, however well written by somebody else, is no substitute for thinking through each step of the process and giving careful consideration to the practical implications of the accompanying activities.

Standard

Trainees use teaching and learning objectives to plan lessons and sequences of lessons, showing how they will assess pupils' learning. They take account of, and support, pupils' varying needs so that girls and boys from all ethnic groups can make good progress (S3.1.2).

Implications for practice

1. The inseparability of planning, teaching and assessment of learning.
2. The need for continuity in learning over a period of time.
3. The importance of teachers' need to know about pupils' academic achievement, potential and limitations.
4. Individual potential, rather than gender, ethnicity or physical condition, as the teacher's prime concern.

Indicative forms of evidence

1. Lesson plans show the relationship between learning objectives, content, teaching strategies and assessment criteria.
2. Lesson plans take account of the content and pupil progress from past lessons and give an indication of links with future lessons.
3. Planning is informed by knowledge of pupils' abilities by discussions with children about their own work, and with reference to school documentation and assessment records.
4. Planning and resourcing ensure that the learning and emotional welfare of all the children is respected and catered for.

Specific forms of evidence

Relationship between objectives, content and assessment...

The lesson content should relate to national guidelines or curriculum requirements and be relevant to children's learning needs. You explain the relevance of the lesson to the children, link it to previous learning and indicate the future lesson direction. You design assessment criteria in such a way that they facilitate a rapid evaluation of pupil learning both during and after the lesson, using evidence from observation of children engaged in tasks, their response to specific questions, the quality of their written work, conversations or group discussion.

Links with previous learning...

You use evidence from past achievements (e.g. pupils' written output) and aptitude (e.g. through careful observation of the way they handle the set tasks) as a basis for lesson planning and organisation, with particular attention to differentiation of subject content for children of varying ability and attention span.

Informed planning...

You make use of school curriculum documents and class assessment information, together with pupils' self-evaluations (reflecting on their own performance) or peer evaluations (reflecting on the performance of a classmate) to guide planning and set appropriate targets for learning.

Concern for the welfare of all children...

You demonstrate that you value all children and are consistent in your encouragement, regardless of gender, ethnicity, physical disability or academic competence. Support for learning is such that children are confident to ask you for advice and share their concerns with you. Group composition and distribution of resources takes positive account of individual needs and you make every effort to actively include every child.

Comment

Planning is not only about establishing learning objectives for children, structuring the teaching and establishing assessment criteria. It is also concerned with the particular needs of children to ensure that every pupil has a fair chance of making optimum progress during the lesson within a secure organisational framework. It is important to consult school documentation and gain as much useful knowledge as possible about the children from host teachers so that planning can be more appropriate and learning more effective. An important component of this process, however, is to take into account the specific welfare of the children in the class, including those from minority ethnic backgrounds and those with special needs. Children not only have to engage with the lesson content but to understand its relevance and feel that they are being given a fair chance to succeed and enjoy learning. Although it is inevitable that you will like some children more than others, your professional responsibility is to strive to ensure that your approach is perceived by each child to be positive, affirming and reasonable. This attitude is expressed in numerous ways, including the way that you speak to different children, allocate resources, use your time and attend to individual needs.

Case study

When Ijaaz walked into Clare's class mid-way through her school experience, she was alarmed to discover that he spoke little English and that the suddenness of his arrival meant that there would be no additional learning support for him for some time. At first she gave nine-year-old Ijaaz some straightforward non-verbal activity sheets, borrowed from the top infant class next door. He seemed mesmerised by everything that was going on and, despite her attempts over the following days to introduce him to a number of trustworthy and friendly children, Ijaaz remained frozen in his own world, choosing to follow at a distance and stand aloof in the playground. Clare worked hard to talk to Ijaaz and involve him in group activities but he only seemed comfortable when seated in front of a computer on his own. The class teacher tried to speak to the parents but Ijaaz went straight off with his little sister after school and efforts to contact the home were fruitless. Clare would like to have spent more time helping her new pupil but the class was extremely lively at the best of times and she had been hard-pressed to cope before his arrival, so she was perplexed about what strategies to employ. As it was her final school experience she was reluctant to admit her anxieties to the mentor in case he retorted by saying: 'If you are going to have your own class in September, you will have to learn to cope with children like Ijaaz', so Clare continued to give him simple tasks requiring little skill or knowledge. It wasn't long before Ijaaz began wandering about the room and sprawling across his desk, ignoring Sue's protestations and directives. It was an experienced classroom helper from the next door class who suggested that Ijaaz might not be disobedient so much as bored. Sue and the teacher decided to start giving him more challenging tasks to do, starting with a three-dimensional jigsaw puzzle and some demanding geometric problems to solve. To their surprise and pleasure Ijaaz's attitude gradually changed from sullen resistance to eagerness over the ensuing days, and he soon began to communicate using simple English that rapidly changed into more sophisticated language use. Such was his progress over the next few weeks that Sue stopped thinking about him as a problem child and included him in her planning as one of the more able pupils in the class. See S3.2.5 and S3.3.5.

Standard

Trainees select and prepare resources, and plan for their safe and effective organisation, taking account of pupils' interests and their language and cultural backgrounds, with the help of support staff where appropriate (S3.1.3).

Where applicable, trainees plan for the deployment of additional adults who support pupils' learning (S3.1.4 in part).

Implications for practice

1. A range of resources to enhance teaching and learning are incorporated into planning.
2. Attention is paid to issues of health and safety in the deployment and use of equipment.
3. Account is taken of the varying needs of children in the selection of resources and the manner in which they are deployed.
4. Support staff are involved in selecting, preparing and using resources.

Indicative forms of evidence

1. Resources are carefully selected and designed to invite children's interest and stimulate their desire to learn.
2. Equipment is safe and works efficiently.
3. The relevance of resources is considered for the diverse range of children in the class.
4. The skills and experience of support staff are utilised in advising about suitable resources and preparing them for use.

Specific forms of evidence

Resources carefully selected...

You ensure that resources are available that fully support the teaching and learning process and the achievement of lesson objectives. Teaching aids are simple, bold, easy to see and straightforward to use. Learning aids are designed and selected so that all children can use them to advantage at their own level of knowledge, understanding and experience. Resources provide instructions or information (e.g. a list of key vocabulary on card) or reinforce learning (e.g. a maths puzzle) or offer a challenge (e.g. materials for creating something in technology). You organise the lesson so that there is direct and easy access to the resources by you and the children.

Safe, efficient equipment...

You have checked equipment carefully before the lesson to ensure its safety and operational efficiency and taken advice from experienced teachers where appropriate. Contingency plans are in place in the event of equipment failure; for example, spare light bulbs are available. You are fully aware of the limits of your expertise and the occasions when specialist assistance will be required. You have checked equipment powered by mains electricity for obvious faults and ensured that the plug has a sticker to show that a qualified electrician has recently examined it.

Appropriate resources for range of children...

In your planning, you have taken account of the age and maturity of the children in selecting and utilising resources, with particular attention to children from minority cultural backgrounds and for whom English is an additional language. Resources are within the capability of all children but you allow more capable children to extend their knowledge and understanding by using, for example, a variety of computer software.

Skills and experience of support staff...

Your planning has made the best use of the skills and expertise of support staff in respect of individual children with outstanding or unusual learning needs. You have made certain, through prior discussion with the person concerned and the class teacher, that the assistant is in a position to exploit the resource fully and understand its potential as a learning aid.

Comment

It is claimed that an individual remembers about one-fifth of what is heard, half of what is seen and heard, but 80 per cent of what is seen, heard and done. Effective use of resources can, therefore, help to transform a mundane lesson into an interesting one, and a good lesson into an excellent one, *providing* they are selected and used with discrimination and care, and engage the children's interest. Resources come in many forms, so it is difficult to specify the way in which they should be used. There are, however, some principles that are important to bear in mind:

(a) *The effort required to produce the resource should never outweigh its potential benefit.* It is far from easy to evaluate the benefits against the costs, but if you are spending more time accessing and/or creating the resource than using it with the children or the children using it for themselves, the effort is probably not worthwhile.

(b) *The resource should assist your teaching, not replace it.* It is tempting to think that the mere provision of a resource will, of itself, transform the lesson. Although an exciting visual resource, for instance, may excite considerable interest and approval, it can also prove to be deleterious. A good example is the use of puppets, which charm and delight children, but if used to excess may also over-stimulate them and create control problems.

(c) *The resource should enhance learning.* The use of computer software to enhance children's learning is sometimes viewed as the answer to a teacher's prayer! It is certainly true that most children love technology and will happily spend hours on task. However, the mere fact that children are occupied does not mean that they are learning anything satisfactory or appropriate. Although it is impossible to guarantee that children will learn what you hope they will, it is important to ask yourself whether the resource will make this more or less likely.

(d) *The resource should be available and ready for use.* Many lessons have been spoiled because essential resources were not in place or difficult for children to utilise. Thus, failure to have produced cards with key vocabulary written on them to support a literacy lesson will obviously result in unnecessary delay while you scramble about looking for card and pens. Similarly, if you overlook the need to fetch equipment from a cupboard in the corridor that is normally open and accessible, you can be sure that it will be locked on this occasion! It is also important to remember that leaving attractive resources within touching distance of the children while you are explaining the activity to them is distracting and a great temptation to little fingers. One trainee teacher was chastened after introducing a lesson with music from *Carnival of the Animals*, only to open the case and discover that someone had borrowed the CD and failed to return it. The trainee had forgotten to check that it was inside before the lesson began or test it in the machine!

(e) *The resource should be suitable for the children you are teaching.* To a certain extent, the use of resources requires a degree of trial-and-error. A mathematics game that one group enjoys immensely can sometimes fail to inspire another. The worksheet that one class enthuses about can be dismissed by another as uninteresting. In addition, there are sometimes cultural factors to consider. For instance, sharing a book about life in a specific area of the world will take on a completely different perspective if there are children sitting in front of you with direct experience of living there. Children and their relatives can be employed as a 'living resource' and greatly enhance a lesson by their first-hand contributions.

Standard

Trainees take part in, and contribute to, teaching teams, as appropriate to the school (S3.1.4 in part).

Implications for practice

1. Willingness for professional dialogue with senior colleagues.
2. Making helpful contributions to discussions and decision-making.
3. Making appropriate contributions to discussions about planning.
4. Limits on contributions that result from inexperience.

Indicative forms of evidence

1. Professionalism is evident throughout the discussions.
2. Comments are well informed and carefully considered.
3. Contributions to planning discussion are pertinent to the purpose of the meeting and provide useful ideas.
4. Contributions to discussion are positive but not self-indulgent.

Specific forms of evidence

Professionalism...

Your approach to teaching and being a teacher in school mirrors that of the teaching staff. You endeavour to draw on your own experiences and insights into school life in the things that you say and do, and express your viewpoint thoughtfully.

Well-informed and considered comments...

Your comments are weighed beforehand, informed by educational opinion and, where appropriate, research findings. You speak knowledgeably about the topic under consideration and can answer colleagues' questions concerning their practical implications. Colleagues acknowledge that your comments enrich the dialogue and are worthy of further consideration.

Pertinent contributions...

You are sensitive to the nature of the occasion when you make your suggestions and comment constructively. Your suggestions take full account of the purpose of the meeting, the degree of formality/informality and the composition of the group. You are able to tailor your words in such a way that they conform to the tenor of the meeting and help to move the agenda forward.

Unassuming contributions...

You are informed about specific and identifiable aspects of school policy in the area under discussion and aware of the impact that your ideas and suggestions might have upon the feelings and working practices of the staff. You offer your comments modestly and carefully, without pretension or promoting a sense of your own importance.

Comment

The days when teachers could operate independently of colleagues and 'keep themselves to themselves' are over. Every head teacher is anxious for the whole staff to cooperate and collaborate in decision-making, implementation of school policies and projects. The best head teachers make sure that every adult (and child) is valued and respected, and given the opportunity to participate in ventures in the belief that a motivated workforce will make best use of its expertise. School situations vary, but it is generally true that even when policies are imposed on schools from central government, staff are expected to work together to ensure that they are implemented in the best interests of the school community.

Case study

Ocean was on her first block of school experience and felt extremely nervous. Although several members of her family were teachers, Ocean was more at ease with children than adults, and was always worried that she might create the impression of being aloof. She particularly enjoyed working with the nursery and reception ages and had been commended for her 'natural' way with children. The head teacher of the placement school believed passionately in collective decision-making and consulted fully with staff at every level. Ocean had strong views on many subjects but hesitated to speak up in public owing to the fact that she coloured quite quickly and easily got flustered. At the first two meetings, she managed to keep a low profile and indicated her involvement and interest by keeping copious notes. This, she reasoned, would not only give a good impression, but would also ensure that she was looking down and not likely to catch the head teacher's eye. However, towards the end of the next meeting and with the whole staff present, the head suddenly looked straight at her and said, 'We haven't heard much from you yet, Ocean. Would you mind sharing some of the things you've been busy writing down?' It was impossible to avoid answering, so Ocean did her best to explain what she thought to be the key points. Even with the encouragement of smiling faces and the affirmative nods of the class teacher, Ocean felt herself blushing furiously and wanted the ground to swallow her up. The head thanked her and commented that she had raised some useful points. Ocean was surprised to hear a murmur of approval from around the room. 'I wonder if you would mind just jotting down a few of those things and passing them on to me. I'll get them typed and circulated to act as a framework for further discussion. Will you have time to do that?' Ocean stuttered her willingness to do so and sat back. She wondered if the head was merely being kind or whether people were genuinely impressed by her ideas. The occasion was a turning point for Ocean. Her notes were indeed used in a subsequent meeting and, although she still fought a constant battle with shyness, her self-esteem rose sharply. Ocean made up her mind to persevere with contributing to the team effort throughout her training and, while never fully at ease in front of other adults, discovered that she had a talent for summarising and clarifying issues on paper. She was overjoyed when her final report included the phrase 'a very good member of the staff team'.

Standard

As relevant to the age range trainees are trained to teach, trainees are able to plan opportunities for pupils to learn in out-of-school contexts, with the help of other staff where appropriate (S3.1.5).

Implications for practice

1. Awareness of the range of out-of-school contexts available for visits and liaison.
2. Awareness of the learning opportunities to be exploited through educational visits.
3. Understanding the links between in-school and out-of-school learning.
4. Consciousness about health and safety factors and their implications.

Indicative forms of evidence

1. Endeavouring to find out about educational outlets (such as museums) in the school locality (see DfES 2002).
2. Having access to information relating to the learning opportunities in different educational outlets.
3. Describing ways in which a child's understanding of class lessons can be enhanced through educational visits.
4. Citing fundamental issues in respect of children's well-being.

Specific forms of evidence

Knowledge of educational outlets...

You know where to access information about the whereabouts and nature of educational establishments and outlets and gain a close knowledge of their location, what they can offer and at what cost.

Information about learning opportunities...

You can explain the educational principles that underpin the value of visits and describe, in detail, ways in which the children's learning can be specifically promoted through visiting a particular location.

Enhancement through visits...

You are able to identify aspects of learning and experiential opportunities that will benefit children and locate the learning that ensues firmly in curriculum documentation, describing ways in which learning can be extended and refined through further activities.

Children's well-being...

You are familiar with the school's health and safety policy and have consulted fully with more experienced teachers about potential hazards and the operation of a risk assessment strategy. You have also considered ways in which organisation can positively influence safety without compromising learning opportunities.

Comment

Educational visits are often the highlight of the year for children. They also place heavy demands upon the teachers concerned in organising and running them (see DfES 2002). Nothing can be left to chance. Every part of the day must be scrutinised with respect to the practical details (such as times of arrival and departure), supervision (such as the allocation of children to adults) and health and safety (such as potential hazards, the frailties of individual children and what to do in an emergency). It is vitally important to liaise with key personnel at the site of the visit or, if it is in an open area (such as a beach), to have made a preliminary visit prior to the outing to ascertain the learning opportunities and limitations. There is a particular need to exercise caution in open areas and spend time before and during the visit in reminding the children about the risks involved and strategies to avoid them. *This briefing is essential in any situation where there is an expanse of water, moving machinery parts or traffic.* All activities that involve an element of possible physical harm (such as climbing) or getting lost (such as orienteering) must be properly supervised by a qualified and experienced instructor. It is useful to have a 'spare' adult during the visit to take photographs and to be available for contacting help should it be necessary. Pupils and adults must be properly briefed, the children given specific tasks to complete during the visit, and account taken of the effect that being out of school might have on excitable children. Although the trip may be sufficient in itself to stimulate curiosity and promote enthusiasm for learning, it is normal to spend time following up the visit in the classroom. As a result, additional resources (such as large paper for displays, adhesive and paints) may have to be ordered in advance of the trip. You may only be an assistant to the teacher as far as the visit is concerned, but you should still be able to verbally communicate your awareness of the issues described above.

Case study

Farhana was enjoying teaching her class of six-year-olds and making good progress with them. She had developed a good working relationship with the two members of the support staff and was looking forward to the class visit to a living museum at a nearby town. The class teacher had involved her in the planning but Farhana had been relieved that he had not asked her to take responsibility for contacting the venue and organising the coach. However, a fortnight before the visit the class teacher broke his arm playing football and was absent from school. Although he was away for less than a week and recovered sufficiently to be present for the outing, his injury limited his ability to finalise the details and lead the party. The head teacher took formal responsibility for the arrangements, but asked Farhana to check that everything was in order and report back to her. Farhana was surprised how much time and effort it took to telephone the museum, confirm the itinerary, follow up the pupils who had not returned their permission slips and organise the adults who were supervising groups of children. Preparing worksheets for the children to use took her ages. On the day, Farhana found that the (now recovered) class teacher stood back and gave her freedom to lead. To her surprise and delight, she relished the task and, despite the pressure of responsibility, rose to the challenge and enjoyed the day. That night, Farhana fell asleep as soon as her head hit the pillow!

Teaching and class management

These standards have been placed ahead of those for Monitoring and Assessment (Section 3.2) to deal with classroom management issues before considering assessment. In practice, effective class management cannot be separated from monitoring children's progress and their behaviour, and assessing their progress throughout and after the lesson. Constant monitoring assists the teacher to shape the lesson in response to children's ongoing learning needs and influences future planning to be more appropriate. Although the heading for this section is teaching and *class* management, teachers also have to be adept at managing the *classroom*. That is, in addition to monitoring children's conduct and curriculum work, they have to take responsibility for the arrangements of tables, location and availability of resources, health and safety aspects and displays. The more you can experience these wider aspects of the role, the better equipped you will be to assume responsibility for your own class and classroom.

Standard

Trainees have high expectations of pupils, build successful relationships centred on teaching and learning and establish a purposeful learning environment where diversity is valued and pupils feel secure and confident (S3.3.1).

Implications for practice

1. Work is suitable and appropriate for the diverse needs of children.
2. Children are encouraged to reflect and comment on their work, to evaluate their progress and learn from their mistakes.
3. Cooperation and collaboration in learning is promoted.
4. A range of strategies are used to encourage children, praise their efforts and provide a purposeful learning environment.

Indicative forms of evidence

1. Children respond positively to the tasks that have been set for them.
2. Children are willing to expose their concerns, admit to their lack of understanding and request help.
3. Children support one another and celebrate each other's achievements.
4. Children receive constructive advice and direction in learning.

Specific forms of evidence

Children respond positively...

The class settles immediately to work with the minimum of fuss. Children engage with the tasks and soon become absorbed in their content. Their questions are for the purpose of clarification and your answers provide them with the information they need to progress. Little monitoring of behaviour is necessary and the calm atmosphere allows you to offer targeted assistance with ease.

Children are willing to expose their concerns...

Children admit when they are concerned or confused, openly seek your advice and are not afraid to ask you for clarification and answers to their questions. If they continue to be uncertain, they don't hesitate to repeat their pleas for help. However, children are not submissive in requesting and receiving answers but are willing to engage in a constructive dialogue with you.

Mutual support and celebration...

Children are spontaneously active in offering one another assistance without being supercilious. They share ideas, collaborate in solving problems and show genuine pleasure at the successes of fellow pupils.

Constructive advice...

You use questions to elicit the children's understanding before giving advice or help. You use appropriate terminology to offer advice and explain things in such a way that children grasp the concept or refine the skill to enhance their learning. Children are able to work more independently as a result of your involvement.

Comment

There is a difference between high and unreasonable expectations. High expectations are about helping children to achieve the best of which they are capable at that time in their lives, taking into account their motivation, relationships and confidence in the subject area. It is clear that a supportive adult (teacher or another) can provide the encouragement, guidance and advice to make this possible. The absence of adult intervention may mean that children fail to reach their potential for the simple reason that they are uncertain about what to do or how to do it, and may become disillusioned as a result. Appropriate adult intervention, on the other hand, can act as a spur for a child who would otherwise have floundered. The benefits to be gained from this kind of positive adult–child relationship are twofold. First, the adult can help children to reach their potential. Second, the child gains confidence from the adult and is willing to share concerns, ask for help and clarify points without fear of being rebuked. Furthermore, a teacher who generates a 'feel good' factor in the classroom is likely to transmit this attitude to the children, who will tend to reflect the teacher's approach in the way they treat one another. One of the principal ways in which a positive learning environment can be achieved is through effective and sensitive feedback to children about the quality of their work. The child who has persevered to achieve something worthwhile (howbeit less impressive than other children) deserves the same level of enthusiastic praise from adults as the more capable pupil. It is important for teachers to avoid falling into the 'yes, but' trap in which children never receive unconditional praise because the imperfections are always pointed out at the same time as the praise. Although children should complete work to their own satisfaction as much as trying to please an adult, the majority of pupils are anxious to receive the teacher's approval. If children hesitate to show the teacher their work for fear of being scolded or regularly told that it is inadequate, it is not conducive to a settled and purposeful environment.

Case study

Gerald had endured more traumas in his eight years of life than some people experience in eighty. Coming from an abusive background, he had been in and out of children's homes and a variety of foster placements. Eventually he was placed back with his natural mother and they lived in a refuge close to the centre of a large town. When Gerald's mother brought him to meet his new teacher it was the seventh school that he had attended. Little wonder that

Gerald was anxious and very reluctant to meet another new set of people and adjust to an unfamiliar situation. Hayley, the trainee, had been getting on well in her teaching and was pleased with the way that the children had responded to her, especially as they were very fond of their regular teacher. In fact, the class teacher had been extremely welcoming and given Hayley her full support. Moreover, there was a lovely ambience to the classroom and the children were responsive and eager to learn. Hayley thought that she must be in heaven! It was, therefore, a shock and slight disappointment when Gerald walked into the room, half-hidden behind his mother, whose strained face betrayed the anxiety that she was feeling. Gerald's passivity and refusal to speak or attempt any work cast a shadow across the bright atmosphere of the room. The class teacher asked Hayley to help him find his feet, but despite her friendly manner and the willingness of other children to take Gerald under their wing, he sat forlornly and spurned their advances. At break time, the teaching assistant, who was normally assigned to another child, managed to coax Gerald away from the security of his seat, show him the toilets (which he steadfastly refused to enter) and take him on to the playground, where he stayed as close to her as possible. During the afternoon, Hayley tried once again to encourage Gerald to participate, but to no avail. The last session was PE in the hall. Gerald did not have any kit and it was with the greatest reluctance that he allowed himself to be ushered along with the other children. Several times he stopped still and refused to move. The class teacher gently but firmly steered him in the right direction but he stood at the side of the hall and stared at the floor. After school had ended, Hayley felt quite miserable and spent nearly an hour talking to the class teacher about the situation. They agreed that Gerald needed time and they would just have to be patient. However, they agreed that they needed a strategy to help him and spent a long time discussing the options. In the end they decided that although ideally they should involve Gerald's mother, she was too vulnerable to be further burdened. Instead, they decided to use a fairly casual tone when speaking to Gerald and to use statements rather than ask questions that might put him under pressure. In addition, they allowed him to help the classroom assistant with some of her basic duties, which Gerald enjoyed. Finally, they took a risk and spoke to the rest of the class about Gerald when he was out of the room, explaining how upset he was feeling about leaving his old school, urging them to be kind and encouraging them to include him in their games. A few children complained that they had tried to be nice to him but that Gerald had been offhand and walked away. However, it was agreed that they would all make a special effort to be kind to Gerald without making it too obvious what was going on behind the scenes! To Hayley's great pleasure and surprise, Gerald began to settle and by the end of the following week became more relaxed and emerged gradually from his silent world. Although he sometimes lapsed and lashed out verbally, Gerald showed that he had a good sense of humour and was capable of being caring. Only at this point did Hayley begin to steer him gently but firmly towards work attached to the formal curriculum and establish her expectations for standards of work. As the class teacher commented, only a contented child is ready to learn.

Standard

Trainees teach clearly structured lessons or sequences of work which interest and motivate pupils (S3.3.3).

Implications for practice

1. Making learning objectives clear to pupils.
2. Using interactive teaching methods.
3. Employing collaborative group work.
4. Promoting active and independent learning.

Indicative forms of evidence

1. Children understand the nature and purpose of the lesson.
2. Teaching involves children through the use of questioning, speculating and creative dialogue.
3. Children can work as a team, each member making a relevant contribution towards the endeavour.
4. Children are capable of discussing their learning, suggesting strategies for improvement and monitoring their own progress.

Specific forms of evidence

Children understand the lesson purpose...

You provide a clear explanation, supported where necessary with a visual reminder, such that children not only claim to understand but are able to tell one another, and you, about the lesson purpose. You locate the explanation securely within the overall framework of learning intentions across a series of lessons and make links with other areas of the curriculum where appropriate.

Teaching involves children closely...

Through a lively, controlled approach, you use a variety of open, closed and speculative forms of questions, invite and value children's contributions, and incorporate their ideas into the threads of your comments. You involve every child by (for instance) requesting that they discuss their ideas briefly with a friend, present them with either/or options and encourage the children to give answers in unison as well as singly. You repeat children's answers of significance to ensure that everyone has heard them and emphasise key learning points for the benefit of all.

Children work as a team...

You monitor the way that children work together, allocate specific responsibilities where necessary and arbitrate disputes. The task is completed more efficiently and of a higher standard than would have been anticipated had the children been working alone. The prior instruction that you have given to the children about helping one another is reflected in the positive learning climate.

Children show independence...

Children can make sensible decisions about their work and priorities. They show initiative and are able to discern between the occasions when they can solve problems for themselves and the occasions when they require support. You are helpful but not intrusive, and willing to discuss problems and potential solutions with the children without being dogmatic. Children are not afraid of failure and view it as part of the learning process.

Comment

Children do not, in the main, take any part in planning lessons. They have little knowledge of the curriculum and even less about targets, national tests and league tables of schools. They turn up each day at school with only a general notion about what the lessons will consist of. They have no idea or interest in the fact that you spent several hours after school erecting a display of their work or sat up half the night assessing their progress. Older children will, of course, have a better grasp of what school is about and sometimes have insights about aspects of school life that would surprise the adults who work there. Nevertheless, for the most part, children respond to, rather than initiate, the things that they are engaged with from day to day. It is therefore up to teachers to explain what is happening, enthuse about the work, offer opportunities for practical tasks and give children information about the usefulness of the endeavour. Involving children in this way provides them with a sense of ownership over the work that is, in itself, a key motivating factor. Children cannot be expected to enjoy everything they do, but they are more likely to be enthusiastic if:

(a) they understand the purpose of the lessons
(b) they are given a chance to work both independently and as part of a group
(c) they have some idea about where the lessons fit into their overall experience of learning.

Case study

Aisha was at a loss to know what to do with her class of ten- and eleven-year-olds. It was the summer term and they were due to move to a new school after the holidays. Not only were there 35 of them, but there was a preponderance of boys and a group of girls who considered themselves to be superior and 'above' doing primary school work. Aisha worked well with the class teacher and assistant. They adopted a positive approach to teaching and encouraged the children at every opportunity, but it was hard going. The class had always been a lively one but now a degree of lethargy had descended which, together with the boisterous boys and fussy group of girls made class management and teaching a considerable challenge. It would have been easy to dismiss them as 'just one of those classes' but Aisha was determined that she was not going to accept the situation. Instead, she agreed with the class teacher that they would modify their plans for the next few weeks and introduce a more collaborative, thematic approach into the work. They decided on a theme called 'A Fairer World For All' and involved the children in the discussions about how they might go about it. At first many of the children did not take things seriously and there were silly suggestions as well as helpful ones. It took perseverance to convince the children that their ideas would, if properly thought through and presented, be considered and included in the project. The children were divided into groups and asked to produce a spider chart of ideas for different areas of the curriculum. Aisha and the class teacher used a study pack on a similar topic as a basis for activities and found a number of websites that provided helpful information. One normally timid boy said that his uncle worked for a charity and volunteered to ask him if he could come into school and tell the class about the plight of people in under-developed countries. As a class they decided that later in the term they would present what they had found to the whole school. Two of the girls offered to bring in some songs, others to design posters. The classroom atmosphere became more constructive and, although the noise level rose and there were times when Aisha wondered if she was losing control of them, she was pleased that a lot of children who were on the margins were beginning to make a contribution. One of the most immediate changes was the way that some of the troublesome children began to speak to one another. Instead of using a surly, confrontational and affected tone, they started to use their normal voices, shared openly and invited others' views. Friction between the disaffected children still surfaced but tended to be of brief duration, as they were more interested in completing the work than pursuing the argument. Despite the effort involved and the occasional setback, the benefits far outweighed the difficulties. The assembly presentation was far from being slick, but it was amusing and well received by the rest of the school. Aisha concluded her time at the school feeling much happier and reassured that teaching was eminently worthwhile when relationships were strong and purposeful, and the children were motivated to learn because they were interested in what they were doing.

Standard

Trainees differentiate their teaching to meet the needs of pupils, including the more able and those with special educational needs, with guidance from an experienced teacher where appropriate (S3.3.4).

Implications for practice

1. Using vocabulary and concepts that can be understood by all pupils.
2. Establishing learning activities appropriate to the range of pupil abilities.
3. Taking particular account of any children with special needs.
4. Asking for guidance from the class teacher, mentor or an experienced colleague.

Indicative forms of evidence

1. Children demonstrate through their answers to questions and comments that they understand what you are saying to them.
2. Children quickly engage with tasks and activities that are set for them.
3. Children with special educational or other needs are catered for with work that provides for success and fulfilment.
4. Planning and teaching take account of general principles and specific advice gained from more experienced practitioners.

Specific forms of evidence

Children demonstrate understanding...

Children not only answer your questions well but offer insightful comments and raise questions of their own. You are aware of misconceptions and misunderstandings and make every effort to correct and rectify them, and to help children to self-correct wherever possible.

Children engage with tasks...

All the children settle to the tasks with minimum fuss and ask very few confirmatory questions about the content of the work. They use resources appropriately and, if working as part of a group, are all involved in collaborating. The atmosphere is settled but vibrant.

Children with special needs catered for...

Your lesson planning is sensitive to the range of needs (including more able) and, where it is appropriate, utilises information contained within an IEP. Work is differentiated and targets for achievement are set accordingly. Children with special educational needs respond positively to the work and make use of adult support without being wholly dependent upon it. They are able to complete tasks within the time frame of the lesson and express pride in their achievements.

Planning takes account of advice...

In planning lessons, evaluating the appropriateness of tasks and assessing children's progress, you take full account of advice from the class teacher and, where necessary, other adults who have specialist knowledge (such as the SENCO). Your lesson evaluations record the impact on teaching and learning that the suggestions have made.

Case study

Khaled was struggling to know how to deal with nine-year-old Catrina. She had transferred from another school (where she had stayed only briefly) at half term and had the shortest concentration span he had ever encountered. Catrina seemed to find it impossible to sit still for more than a few minutes before she was standing up and wandering around the room, asking in a penetrating voice for help and advice, or recounting something she had seen on television. Her written presentation was untidy and every task was carried out with lightning speed, following which she would put her books away, sit upright in her chair with arms folded for thirty seconds before re-commencing her travels. No other child befriended her and she did not actively seek companionship. Catrina struggled to grasp concepts and asked so many questions of Khaled that he almost felt under siege. The class teacher was also struggling to suggest activities that Catrina could cope with and ways to occupy the available time without the accompanying disruption. The head teacher and SENCO both agreed that Catrina's problem was as much to do with confidence and organisation of her time as it was with behaviour. In fact, they all agreed that Catrina was not so much 'naughty' as bewildered and confused, lacking the necessary skills and self-discipline to conform, so Khaled and the class teacher, advised by the SENCO, decided on an eight-fold strategy:

(a) To give Catrina space and time to settle and not inadvertently label her as a troublemaker by telling her off publicly where it was possible to use a more discreet method.
(b) To spend a few minutes each day talking to her about her interests, creating trust and building up a better profile of Catrina as an individual.
(c) To provide her with straightforward tasks that did not require much interpreting and could be completed rapidly.
(d) To give feedback that would be positive and approving whenever possible, especially when she persevered with her work.
(e) To give Catrina some status among her peers by being given a special job to do. (They decided to make armbands for her and another girl saying 'Librarian'. Catrina faithfully tidied the books for the next week or so before the novelty wore off but it gave opportunity for Khaled to approve her actions and make a fuss of her.)
(f) To make a special effort to help Catrina with basic tasks such as keeping her tray tidy and walking rather than scurrying about.
(g) To have a simple 'star chart' for Catrina with four categories: (1) I look after my things, (2) I speak quietly, (3) I walk carefully, (4) I work slowly.
(h) To invite Catrina's mother to meet with them for five minutes every Thursday after school to review progress.

Catrina's attitude did not change overnight, but the close and consistent attention she received helped her behaviour to become less manic and she began to take an interest in her schoolwork, as previously her mind had been too full of hidden fears to make it a priority. Khaled pondered the fact that children cannot be expected to learn and conform when they are anxious and emotionally vulnerable. Catrina continued to progress in fits and starts but remained a challenge for the staff in the school.

Standard

Trainees are able to support those who are learning English as an additional language, with the help of an experienced teacher where appropriate (S3.3.5).

Trainees take account of the varying interests, experiences and achievements of boys and girls, and pupils from different cultural and ethnic groups, to help pupils make good progress (S3.3.6).

Trainees recognise and respond effectively to equal opportunities issues as they arise in the classroom by challenging stereotyped views, bullying or harassment, following relevant policies and procedures (S3.3.14).

Implications for practice

1. Encouraging pupils to develop and extend their own interests where possible.
2. Ensuring that boys and girls have full access to curriculum opportunities.
3. Providing support materials suitable for children for whom English is not a first language.
4. Valuing the breadth of cultural heritage in the class.

Indicative forms of evidence

1. Children are encouraged to pursue their specific interests within the general remit of the subject content of the lesson or lessons.
2. Every member of the class is given equal access to resources, activities and equipment.
3. Visual aids, worksheets, displays and verbal information take account of different language needs.
4. Children are actively encouraged to contribute information, insights and perspectives from their culture.

Specific forms of evidence

Children pursue interests...

You promote the belief among the children that their out-of-school interests and knowledge provide an important contribution to the curriculum. You encourage children to share their knowledge and insights about specific areas of learning for the benefit of the class. You establish problem-solving and investigative activities so that all children have opportunity to strengthen areas of interest, explore their own understanding and draw from their experiences.

Equal access...

You ensure through a rota or use of an assistant that every child has a fair and reasonable opportunity to engage with the full range of learning opportunities, while taking careful account in planning to differentiate for individual needs. You are careful to see that more assertive children do not receive undue attention and favour.

Language needs...

You make allowance in your speed of delivery, articulation and vocabulary for children who do not have a complete grasp of English, taking care not to patronise or trivialise. Where necessary, you involve teaching assistants to help with native tongue language use and try, where possible, to include the range of languages represented in the class on displays and instructions.

Cultural perspectives...

You encourage children to talk about their culture and, with guidance from the class teacher, invite well-informed contributions from people outside the school. You are careful, within the boundaries of school-wide agreed procedures, not to unintentionally create unease by insisting that children behave and respond in ways that are culturally offensive. You ensure that stories, examples, identification of heroic figures and historical perspectives are drawn from a variety of world perspectives and that ethnic diversity is valued.

Case study

Five-year-old Zango had recently arrived with his parents from a Central African state. His father was undertaking advanced study at the nearby university and the family would be domiciled in temporary accommodation for the following year at least. Zango spoke quite good English but preferred to communicate in his tribal language. He was bright and eager to learn but had no experience of formal schooling, having been educated privately in his home country. Harmony found the situation challenging but exciting and enjoyed being placed in a situation that had such diversity. Although Zango was shy at first, he soon began to gain confidence and, although he found it hard to comply with some of the classroom procedures, demonstrated that he had a nimble mind and learned quickly. Harmony enjoyed having Zango in the class and, when she heard that his father had been a tribal chief in his home country, thought that it would be a good idea to ask him if he would come and share something with the children for their 'All About Me' project. After checking with the head teacher, the class teacher encouraged Harmony to make the arrangements. After several letters and a face-to-face meeting, Zango's father not only agreed to come into the school, but offered to bring with him a troupe that specialised in native costume, music and dance. The event was a great success for, after hearing about the proposal, the head teacher suggested that it would be appropriate for the whole school to share the experience if Zango's father would agree, which he duly did. As part of the follow-up, Harmony was given the email address of a school in Zango's hometown and before she finished the placement, she was able to establish links with it. The project took off, and such was the enthusiasm generated by the partnership that other, similar events were soon being planned.

Standard

Trainees organise and manage teaching and learning time effectively (S3.3.7).

Trainees organise and manage the physical teaching space, tools, materials, texts and other resources safely and effectively, with the help of support staff where appropriate (S3.3.8).

Implications for practice

1. Planning for lessons takes account of what is achievable in the time available.
2. Planning takes account of the physical space required for a successful lesson.
3. Lesson management allows adequate time for each lesson phase.
4. Resources and equipment are prepared and ready for use.

Indicative forms of evidence

1. The lesson starts and finishes on time and children cover most or all of the set work.
2. Classroom furniture is organised in such a way that resources are accessible and there is adequate space for the activities to be carried out.
3. The lesson plan includes a time allocation for each section of the lesson, including introduction and conclusion.
4. Resources are in good condition, checked for safety and correctly used.

Specific forms of evidence

Starting and finishing on time...

The lesson begins promptly and children are quickly on task. The lesson proceeds in an orderly but positive manner and time is available at the end for a summary phase and clearing up. There is a sense of purpose to the proceedings without them being hurried.

Space allocation...

You have organised where the children sit such that they all have good visibility and do not need to twist or sit unnaturally to see what is happening. The room is well lit and children can work comfortably without straining their eyes. The amount of space is appropriate for the task or activity and there is adequate space for the children to move and have access to resources without inconveniencing others. For instance, practical activities are not cramped into a small area causing difficulty when using adhesive, scissors and rulers.

Lesson phases...

Your lesson is well balanced and contains an introduction, mid-section (including tasks, discussion or collaborative problem solving) and a summary phase. You spend time on the introduction, reminding children of what has gone before, eliciting what they remember through question-and-answer and highlighting key points. You employ a variety of learning strategies, including collaboration where work together is desirable. You take account of the fact that some children may complete tasks more rapidly than expected by preparing some extension activities. The plenary is used to reinforce learning, share findings, to celebrate achievements and point the way ahead.

Accessibility of resources...

You have prepared in advance both consumable and non-consumable resources with the aid of an assistant as appropriate. The lesson proceeds smoothly because there is no time wasted in organising resources or repairing faulty equipment. Children have been given suitable training in its use and reminded about possible hazards. Items are put away correctly and sensibly.

Case study

Bernard had always struggled with time management. He was invariably 'last minute' with completing assignments and in previous school placements had been warned that he needed to spend more time updating his teaching file and maintaining records of pupil progress. Bernard was a naturally gifted teacher and excelled in front of the class but his tutors felt that he spent too much time helping with after-school activities and too little researching lessons. On Bernard's final placement he was in a school that had been in special measures. A new head teacher had been appointed and she had decided that one strategy for lifting standards was to insist on more systematic lesson preparation and record-keeping. The staff had been far from happy about the additional administrative load but reluctantly agreed that it was beneficial. They felt that they had little choice, as the new head was not afraid to confront them if she believed that they were reneging on the agreed policy. Bernard found that he had no option but to knuckle down, sort out his file and spend an adequate amount of time on preparation. He was sensible enough to respond positively and reduce his extraneous commitments, while discussing the issue of time management with the mentor. Although Bernard secretly felt that the prescriptive demands of the head teacher restricted his ability to be innovative, he had to admit that the discipline it imposed on him helped considerably once he was in post and was faced with the full range of class and school responsibilities.

Standard

Trainees set high expectations for pupils' behaviour and establish a clear framework for classroom discipline to anticipate and manage pupils' behaviour constructively, and promote self-control and independence (S3.3.9).

Implications for practice

1. Expectations of pupil behaviour are made explicit.
2. Learning is organised to facilitate smooth lesson management.
3. Discipline strategies are employed consistently.
4. Children are encouraged to take responsibility for their own actions.

Indicative forms of evidence

1. Expectations are explained plainly to the children with reference to agreed rules and procedures.
2. Children are grouped appropriately and given clear learning targets.
3. Inappropriate behaviour is dealt with in a measured and decisive manner, in proportion to the nature of the misdemeanour.
4. Children are helped to think carefully about the nature and consequences of their actions.

Specific forms of evidence

Expectations explained...

You allocate regular times to explore with the children what is acceptable behaviour and address directly the implications of the class rules. You discuss with the children how to behave under particular circumstances, stressing positive and appropriate action. Your tone is firm, but in answer to children's queries your answers show them that you are fair and reasonable. In class situations you remind the children of the rules from time to time.

Effective organisation...

You decide in advance of each lesson the way in which children will be grouped for working or whether you want them to work independently. You ensure that the lesson is better able to flow along by considering carefully the resource and practical implications, the appropriateness of learning targets and the level of support children need for success. You give instructions unambiguously, taking full account of factors that might impair their understanding, such as immaturity, language difficulties and poor memory. You involve learning assistants as appropriate, making sure that they are fully briefed.

Dealing with inappropriate behaviour...

You affirm appropriate behaviour and make regular approving comments when children are sensible. You maintain a firm grip on the numerous ebbs and flows of classroom life by making it clear to the children that you are aware of what is happening and the acceptability or otherwise of their actions. Your responses are in proportion to the event and you remain calm, even under provocation. In all circumstances, you concentrate on the nature of the misdemeanour and not on the personality or character of the child. Where necessary you refocus the children's attention or change the lesson tempo to discourage poor behaviour. On the rare occasions that sanctions are necessary, you apply them consistently and without rancour.

Inculcating self-discipline...

You insist that children face up to their responsibilities by clarifying that every action has a consequence and put the onus on them to justify their decisions. You do not permit a climate of blame, evasion or denial to develop. You do not allow children to trivialise the impact or seriousness of their behaviour by jesting or being flippant. You include other adults (such as the class teacher) in your deliberations about what constitutes acceptable behaviour. You create an atmosphere of mutual respect through modelling good character and agreed boundaries. You regularly involve children in thinking through the implications of their behaviour and promote constructive strategies for addressing behaviour issues with the children and establishing accepted norms.

Case study

Natalie had been placed in a nursery class and enjoyed working with the three- and four-year-old children but struggled to cope with Ethel, who exhibited poor self-control and sometimes became very disruptive in the unit. Ethel's parents were involved with the school in devising strategies to help their daughter become more compliant but they blamed her behaviour on food additives and said that as both of them worked long hours, they could not spend as much time with her as they would like. Natalie secretly thought that the parents' lack of willingness to insist on standards of behaviour in the home was a major source of Ethel's difficulties in school. One of the issues that emerged as a result of the problem about food additives was that Ethel's meals varied considerably from all the other children and she clearly resented the fact. She would eat very little and, while the other children sat nicely and enjoyed their food, would jump down from the table and play with the toys, which was not allowed. Natalie expressed her concerns about Ethel to the teacher, who explained that the staff had agreed that on balance it was better to ignore the behaviour and maintain the peace rather than to insist on Ethel remaining at the table and having to deal with the subsequent tantrums. Natalie was uneasy about this compromise and asked the teacher if she could try a different strategy of talking to Ethel about her behaviour and encouraging her to understand that her actions were not helpful and were breaking the agreed rule about staying at the table. However, whenever Natalie raised the subject with her, Ethel was uncooperative and sulked, so a new plan was devised. Whenever Ethel was sensible at the table she would be given first choice of choosing her favourite toy or game in the afternoon, but when she broke the rule and refused to return to the table, she was made to have a rest-time with the younger children. Ethel hated the rest-time and made a terrible fuss at first but gradually realised that if she conformed, she would benefit, and if she deliberately broke the rule she would not. After much perseverance and numerous setbacks, Natalie was pleased and relieved that Ethel began to do what she was told at lunch times (most of the time) and her general level of cooperative behaviour improved, too.

Standard

Trainees use ICT effectively in their teaching (S3.3.10).

Implications for practice

1. Opportunities for use of ICT in lesson plans.
2. Children learning general computing skills, including the use of appropriate terminology.
3. Selection of appropriate software for subject and topic areas.
4. Children using electronic sources appropriate to their age and ability.

Indicative forms of evidence

1. The ways in which ICT can assist learning are made explicit in plans and explanations.
2. Lessons are designed to allow children a measure of independence in the use of ICT equipment and encouragement to employ the correct terms when doing so.
3. Software supports knowledge and conceptual development.
4. Children know how to access information and make considered choices about its value for their learning.

Specific forms of evidence

Planning for ICT-assisted learning...

Your lesson plans incorporate ICT opportunities and identify when and how they can be used. Computers and/or other hardware are checked and ready for use. You have taken account of the practical implications for incorporation of ICT, in particular the monitoring of usage and equality of opportunity. You ensure that appropriate support is available for less confident children through clearly produced instructions (written/diagrammatic) or the availability of well-informed and properly briefed support staff.

Teaching ICT skills...

You are capable of contributing towards teaching children computing skills in a computer suite or in a classroom situation, and recognise the need to differentiate according to children's skill level and experience. Your lesson plans take account of children's existing ICT skills and where they might be utilised for common benefit.

Appropriate software...

You are able to justify your selection of software appropriate to the subject area or topic such that children are able to extend their learning as a result and do not require a lot of adult attention in doing so.

Accessing information...

You have knowledge about using electronic mail, the Internet, digital cameras, electronic whiteboards, and recording and reporting pupils' progress. You can assist children in using electronic means for the purpose of extending their knowledge and understanding; in particular, accessing the National Grid for Learning (NGfL).

Comment

The use of ICT in learning varies considerably from school to school. There has been a considerable increase in the scope and range of technology available for children and teachers but not necessarily an increase in the extent to which it is used. There are three principal reasons for this trend. First, teachers recognise that ICT is not the sole solution to the challenges that face them on a daily basis. The availability of advanced technology has made possible the production of diagrams, artistic designs, spreadsheets, and so forth, and reduced the time that it would once have taken to assemble data. It has also acted as a motivating factor for many children. However, ICT has to be organised and managed as carefully as any other resource. It is prone to technical failure and requires regular adult supervision. Ensuring that all children have reasonable access to resources is also far from easy to monitor. Second, time spent on machines (especially computers) does not mean that quality learning is taking place. Teachers have found that it is possible for children to achieve little, despite being occupied in front of a machine for long periods of time. Third, technology can detract from the first-hand experiences that young children, in particular, need to extend their understanding and increase their social awareness. ICT is best seen as a support for, and enhancement of, children's learning experiences, rather than a substitute for them.

Standard

Trainees can take responsibility for teaching a class or classes for a sustained and substantial period of time. They are able to teach across the age and ability range for which they are trained (S3.3.11).

Implications for practice

1. Lesson planning covers consecutive lessons.
2. Teaching experience is gained across KS1/KS2 or foundation/KS1 range.
3. Teaching experience involves dealing with a full range of ability.
4. Teaching approaches reflect the age and maturity of the children.

Indicative forms of evidence

1. Learning outcomes relate to a series of lessons rather than single, isolated ones.
2. Whole-class teaching takes place with a mixed ability group of children.
3. A substantial period of time is spent in two key stages/foundation stage.
4. Teaching methods and strategies allow children in the age phase to engage meaningfully with the work and extend their learning.

Specific forms of evidence

Learning across a series of lessons...

You identify specific learning objectives and assessment criteria relevant to individual lessons, and general objectives relevant to a series of lessons, informed by the school's medium-term plans. Pupil progression is allowed for through appropriate differentiation of the tasks and activities, and you are able to accommodate some of the spontaneous learning opportunities that arise.

Teaching mixed ability...

You regularly teach consecutive lessons to the whole class and differentiate according to the children's learning needs in one of three ways:

(a) By setting tasks of varying conceptual demands to groups of differing abilities.
(b) By grading tasks in such a way that children work through them consecutively at their own pace.
(c) By setting a similar task or activity to all the children but assessing the outcomes based on your knowledge of individual capability.

Time in two stages...

You teach consecutive lessons/sessions to children in each of two key stages/foundation stage, though not necessarily in the same school. The amount of time that you spend with an age phase allows you to adjust your teaching approach to suit their specific needs. You are able to explain to a tutor or mentor how your teaching is modified to take account of the particular learning needs of different year groups. You use teachers who work in different age phases as models for good practice and have opportunity to discuss teaching strategies with them.

Modifying approach for different ages...

You teach through a variety of approaches, including direct transmission, collaborative group work, exploratory methods and investigation, and the use of visual or kinaesthetic means, according to the age and ability of the class. Younger children are given extensive opportunity to play, cooperate through joint activities, talk with one another about the activities, express themselves in a variety of media and record findings in different ways. Older children are given opportunity to discuss and debate, raise questions, follow instructions systematically, use ICT to tabulate results, explore the implications of decisions and master subject-specific vocabulary. Your speed of delivery, use of questions, terminology, explanations, tasks and summaries reflect the particular needs of the class and their ages. For example, you speak more slowly and deliberately when addressing younger children.

Case study

Lesley enjoyed working with her preferred age range of younger primary children but was extremely uneasy at the prospect of teaching the Year 5 class to which she had been allocated for the latest school placement. For a start, she was quite short in stature and looked young for her age, so much so that in her previous school a parent mistook her for one of the Year 6 children! Furthermore, all her pre-course experience had been helping her mother in a local nursery and working for a short spell in her old village primary school with reception age children. Even her previous placement had been with a foundation/Year 1 group in an infant school, so opportunity to see teachers at work with KS2 children had been restricted to two brief visits to the nearby junior school. It was therefore with some relief that she found the new placement school to be welcoming and the classroom environment to be relaxed. The class teacher tried to reassure Lesley that everything would work out, and the children seemed to go out of their way to show that they were decent and fair-minded. During the first few days Lesley felt tense and was not able to relax or eat properly, but she quickly acclimatised and began to take stock of some of the differences between teaching older and younger primary. At the end of the first week, she reviewed her list of things that characterise a KS2 classroom:

(a) Classes tend to be larger than in KS1.
(b) The pace of classroom life is rapid, sometimes verging on frenetic.
(c) Teachers speak quite quickly to the children and expect that they will understand first time.
(d) Children are noisier than younger ones and less inclined to become upset, though occasional emotional outbursts are not unknown.
(e) Tensions associated with friendship patterns are pronounced.
(f) The line of demarcation between different lessons is quite rigid.
(g) Children work unaided for longer and ask a lot of questions about the teacher's expectations for them.
(h) Many children prefer to be independent of the teacher.
(i) Children often express their ideas with conviction and deep feeling.
(j) Activities in core subjects nearly always have specified outcomes that are pre-determined by the teacher.
(k) The range of ability is extremely wide, especially in mathematics.
(l) There is a considerable hiatus between mature girls and less mature boys.
(m) The topics of conversation between boys and girls are markedly different.
(n) Teachers do a lot of direct teaching.
(o) There are times when a considerable amount of humour and banter is exchanged and times when learning is formally monitored and the teacher is very strict.
(p) There is strong rivalry and competition between children, especially the more able boys.
(q) Friendship patterns are well established and highly significant for the children.
(r) There is more specialist teaching.

(s) Teachers collaborate for planning more than they do in the actual teaching.
(t) Teachers require a high level of subject knowledge if they are teaching more able children in core subjects.
(u) Cheekiness is more prevalent and some children conceal their ignorance by being silly.

Lesley noted that younger children, by contrast, require greater nurturing and attention to basic skills. The reception age children that she had worked with were, on the whole, more easily satisfied and prone to get upset rather than naughty if they did not understand the work or were failing to cope. When Lesley began taking more responsibility for planning work, she found that the ability level was so wide in the Year 5 class that she had to differentiate questions and tasks carefully. She also had to develop activities that allowed children to remain self-sufficient, owing to the fact that there were fewer adult helpers than she was used to having in KS1. The pace of the opening phase of the lesson took her aback initially and she felt as if she had been through a spin-drier! At the same time, it was exhilarating to deal with a large number of enthusiastic juniors, most of whom were willing to stretch their arms another few centimetres into the air in the hope of being chosen to answer a question! Lesley took some time to get used to the vociferousness of many children who, instead of sulking like younger ones tended to do, voiced their opinions loudly. At first Lesley misinterpreted their behaviour and thought that they were about to run amok; gradually she realised that older children have not only louder voices but a wider vocabulary and firmer opinions. She was privately intimidated by one or two of the boys who seemed to have an answer for everything, including why they should do what they wanted and not what she wanted them to do! However, she was pleased that the children could do so much more for themselves than their younger contemporaries and she was less physically tired at the end of the day. Lesley was surprised that some children had such gaps in their understanding and knowledge. This was particularly pronounced in reading and use of ICT. In the more creative subjects (e.g. artwork) a few children would revert to immature techniques unless specifically taught more sophisticated ones. Lesley still felt more at home with younger children but benefited from her time working with the Year 5 children in two ways. First, she had a better idea about the direction in which the KS1 children were 'heading' in their learning and a firmer grasp of what infant age children needed to know and master if they were to prosper at KS2. Second, she had observed and been involved in handling a different range of teaching skills and methods, some of which she could apply to her teaching at KS1. Ironically, Lesley's first teaching post after qualifying was in a Year 3/4 class, where she coped admirably.

Standard

Trainees can provide homework and other out-of-class work, which consolidates and extends work carried out in the class and encourages pupils to learn independently (S3.3.12).

Implications for practice

1. Homework/out-of-class work has to be appropriate to the age and ability of the pupil.
2. Homework/out-of-class work has to relate closely to learning that takes place in school.
3. Homework/out-of-class work has to be realistic and manageable.
4. Homework/out-of-class work has to be monitored and assessed.

Indicative forms of evidence

1. Homework tasks are differentiated in such a way that pupils can cope unaided if necessary.
2. Tasks are directly related to in-school learning and contribute towards the same learning outcomes.
3. Pupils are able to complete tasks without the need for sophisticated resources.
4. Formative feedback is offered to pupils with suggestions for improvement.

Specific forms of evidence

Differentiated tasks...

You allocate different tasks based on children's abilities or you give the same task to all children such that they are all able to engage with it at their own level and make observable progress.

Links to prior learning...

The tasks that you allocate provide consolidation and extension opportunities that might have been available in school had time permitted and, for the most part, are rooted in situations that are familiar to the children. You convince the children that the homework is supplementary to, and not separate from, their regular work.

Tasks require minimum resources...

Children have resources immediately at hand or you provide them. Tasks should not rely on the availability of sophisticated equipment. Parents should not be expected to produce resources in such a way that might financially embarrass or inconvenience them or their children. For example, geography homework should not require the use of a world atlas as some parents may feel obliged to go out and purchase one so that their children were not disadvantaged.

Feedback to pupils...

You scrutinise or discuss the homework with the children and comment on the basis of clearly understood criteria. Groups or individuals are given specific targets for learning whenever possible. In the case of an identical task for all children, you make general comments about the overall quality of homework tasks with indicators about improvements or implications for learning.

Comment

Homework is only useful if it builds on previous school-based work or begins to open up new avenues of learning. Some homework tasks involve finishing off incomplete work from the day; however, this penalises slower workers and does little to extend the more able. The best type of homework is in the form of mini-projects, whereby children are given a range of tasks and activities covering a number of curriculum areas to complete over a period of time. Although it should be possible for children to do their homework unaided, it is most effective when there is a role for adults in the process. For younger children, additional reading, supported by an adult if possible, is frequently used as a homework task. Homework can provide a starting point for discussion and sharing experiences, the very heart blood of learning for children of all ages. See also comments under S1.4.

Teaching: Monitoring and Assessment

Standard

Trainees make appropriate use of a range of monitoring and assessment strategies to evaluate pupils' progress towards planned learning objectives, and use this information to improve their own planning and teaching (S3.2.1).

Trainees monitor and assess as they teach, giving immediate and constructive feedback to support pupils as they learn. They involve pupils in reflecting on, evaluating and improving their own performance (S3.2.2).

Implications for practice

1. Monitoring is a key element of the formative assessment process.
2. Assessment should contribute to learning.
3. Assessment criteria should be established alongside learning objectives.
4. Future planning and teaching should take account of both formative and summative assessments.

Indicative forms of evidence

1. Children are provided with constructive feedback during lessons.
2. Pupils' work is regularly assessed against agreed norms and children are encouraged to evaluate their own progress.
3. Assessment criteria match the purpose of the lesson or lessons.
4. Overall assessment of learning directly influences future lesson design.

Specific forms of evidence

Constructive feedback...

You affirm progress and offer support when appropriate, but also encourage children to think for themselves and become independent learners through prompts, speculative questions and reframing of ideas. You remind children about the lesson purpose and offer guidance such that this is more likely to be achieved. However, you also acknowledge and value instances where children have selected alternative strategies and are willing to think creatively. Where misunderstanding or poor grasp of concepts is evident, you spend time identifying the source of the problem and offering further explanation. You take opportunities to publicly commend perseverance and innovation.

Assessment improving learning...

You provide information to children specific enough to help them to rectify mistakes, reconfigure their ideas and improve their understanding. You invite children to comment on their own efforts and, where appropriate, teach them the skills necessary to offer constructive criticism of each other's work. Your feedback acts as a spur to achievement and not as a depressant. Children eagerly seek your help in the expectation that they will be given fresh hope and direction.

Assessment criteria...

The criteria reflect the learning objectives for the lesson and can be located in the overarching objectives for the series of lessons. The criteria are designed in such a way that it is possible to make a rapid evaluation of children's learning by examination of their written output, their comments and questions, and their ability to cope with the various challenges that you set them.

Future planning and teaching...

You utilise information from summative and formative assessments to modify future learning objectives, teaching approach and the tasks and activities to support and enhance understanding. You use the comments from your annotated lesson plans to establish new targets for your own learning as well as the children's. For example, you may recognise from the large number of questions from the children requesting additional explanation about the work that you need to be more careful in the way that you introduce the lesson. Again, the speed with which more able children complete tasks may indicate that a greater degree of differentiation is needed in the tasks that you set for them.

Comment

Assessment has little to do with meeting the artificially constructed targets that the school, local education authority or governments establish. It has everything to do with helping children to enjoy learning and fulfil their potential, aided by the best possible guidance from adults. Ask any child of any age in any class who is the best at reading, maths and drawing, etc. and you are likely to receive an accurate answer. How do they know? Quite simply, because all children are aware from the earliest age of who is coping with the class work and who is not coping. They are also sensitive to adult expectations and the implications of success and (horrible word to use of a child) failure. If children feel that the *only* thing that matters to teachers and the outside world is test scores, education is reduced to a clinical formula of grades and positions in league tables. If, on the other hand, children view test scores as one way among many of evaluating progress, they have hope that their other qualities, such as kindness, decency and the ability to work as part of a team, are valued. Of course, the ideal is that children succeed in both areas: academic and social. In practice, the assessment criteria that you establish in regard to the broad lesson objectives should be based on two questions: (a) What am I trying to help the children to achieve during this lesson or lessons? (b) What evidence will inform me about the extent to which I have been successful? Whereas it is possible to gain a general 'feel' for how successful the lesson appears to have been (through observing the children's responses and their application to task) the question of how individual children have fared requires more careful attention. This level of information about children can only be gained over a period of time and should not be based on a single piece of work. Nevertheless, as a trainee teacher you should try to evaluate every lesson, in terms both of its general impact and of the progress of individuals. Your sensitivity and interest in the progress of individual children through formative feedback, careful explanation, patient persistence and celebrating achievement at every level will make assessment an ally, not an enemy.

Standard

Trainees are able to assess pupils' progress accurately using, as relevant, assessment frameworks or objectives from the national strategies. They may have guidance from an experienced teacher where appropriate (S3.2.3).

Implications for practice

1. Assessments need to be accurate.
2. Assessment is useful only if it contributes to learning.
3. Knowledge of the National Curriculum and Foundation Stage profile is important.
4. Advice from more experienced teachers should be sought when making assessments.

Indicative forms of evidence

1. Assessments can be verified by reference to evidence.
2. Assessment provides information that helps to establish targets for learning.
3. National frameworks are used as a general guide to pupil progress in numeracy and literacy.
4. Discussion with teachers or tutors reveals a grasp of the principles and practicalities associated with national testing and profiling.

Specific forms of evidence

Verification of assessments...

You use a range of evidence about individuals that you have accumulated, some of which is quantitative (such as recording formal test scores) and some of which is qualitative (such as noting key points that emerge from conversations with children about their work) to inform decisions about attainment. You analyse selected work samples to support or confirm your assessments. You develop 'assessment profiles' of children drawn from observations and daily contact with them, team discussions about their social progress and samples of work including, where appropriate, photographs of paintings, models and large-scale projects. You are capable of defending your evaluations of attainment by reference to specific work samples.

Assessment informing target setting...

Specific information that you glean from formative and summative assessment evidence allows for an informed discussion with individual children about their priorities for learning, including good work that can be further improved and weaker work that can be strengthened. The targets are such that it is possible to monitor progress over time. For example, a target might be to 'access more information electronically' rather than merely to 'find out more information'. Whereas success in the first target can be verified quite easily, success in the second cannot.

Use of national frameworks...

You demonstrate a working knowledge of national assessment guidance and procedures relevant to the age group you teach and where children's work and/or attitude to learning matches the attainment levels of the NC and/or foundation stage profile. You work alongside the resident teacher to prepare children for formal and preparatory tests including, where appropriate, coaching and optional end-of-year assessments. In consultation with an experienced teacher you undertake 'levelling' of individual pieces of children's work against the national subject criteria (attainment targets). Where possible, you gain experience assisting with the administration of national tests.

Consultation with host teachers...

You are able to hold constructive discussions with experienced teachers about the preparation for, and conducting of tests. You show by your questions and comments that you have insights into the emotional, practical, social and academic issues associated with testing. Thus:

(a) *Emotionally*... tests are enjoyed by most of the able children, but may create anxiety among the anxious and less able children.
(b) *Practically*... preparations for tests usually involve alterations to the timetable and methods of teaching, especially in the weeks preceding the test.
(c) *Socially*... parents and the community are extremely interested in the outcomes of tests and place great store by numerical scores.
(d) *Academically*... test scores (in particular) and profiles (to a lesser extent) provide valuable information about some (but not all) aspects of a child's intellect, ability to cope with formal situations and strengths in different subject areas.

Case study

Of all the children in her class, Janice found Imogene to be the biggest puzzle. Over the three weeks that she had been placed in the Year 4 class, Janice felt that Imogene, who was quite new to the school, was the one child whose capability she had been unable to understand adequately. In the unfortunate absence of the regular class teacher for the previous two weeks, Janice had felt obliged to assume far more responsibility for the class than she had anticipated and she was unable to ask directly about the 'mixed messages' that Imogene was giving. At one level Imogene was articulate and eager to please; on other occasions, she was passive and almost dreamlike in her attitude. Imogene presented her work poorly and made frequent careless errors, but her reading showed strong evidence of high order skills. To confuse matters further, Imogene's handwriting and spelling were irregular and inconsistent. Janice just didn't know what to make of her and struggled to assess her progress. However, records from Imogene's previous school indicated that she was capable of high achievement and had scored well in the end-of-year tests in Year 3, particularly English comprehension. After giving several spelling tests to the class, Janice noticed that Imogene tended to make mistakes with simpler words, yet correctly spell the harder ones. After taking advice from the mentor, Janice found time to sit with Imogene and talk to her in some depth about her work. At first, Imogene seemed reluctant to reveal her thoughts, but after a while she began to talk freely about the fact that she had always been a bit clumsy and struggled to keep her writing neat. She admitted to finding maths difficult and did not ask too many questions because she was afraid of looking silly. She loved reading and would prefer to look at books, especially storybooks, more than anything else. To Janice's surprise, Imogene was clear about her weaker areas and even had some constructive ideas about how she might go about remedying them. They agreed that one obvious area for improvement was Imogene's presentation of work. The second broad target was to take more care over the spelling of simple words. Imogene expressed a desire to spend more time working with some of the more compliant children as, being quite new, she did not have a 'proper' friend and tended to be lumped with other fringe class members, some of whom were work-shy. Following the conversation, Janice's relationship with Imogene was stronger and, when the class teacher returned the following week, he commented on how much more settled and purposeful Imogene seemed to be. Janice reflected that although she had a number of misgivings about the emphasis on formal testing and setting targets for learning, she had to admit that the information from the end-of-year tests and in-class tests helped to shape the agenda and focus attention on key aspects of Imogene's academic work. Janice was also surprised to discover how powerfully the social element of classroom life affected children's attitude and motivation. From the moment that Imogene made close friends with another new girl who arrived in the class later the same week, she settled to her work attentively. Although Imogene continued to make somewhat erratic progress, Janice was pleased that the assessment process had made a positive contribution towards improving her learning.

Standard

Trainees identify and support more able pupils, those who are working below age-related expectations, those who are failing to achieve their potential in learning, and those who experience behavioural, emotional and social difficulties. They may have guidance from an experienced teacher where appropriate (S3.2.4).

Implications for practice

1. Accurate assessment is made of children's present attainment through discussions with teachers.

2. A distinction is made between children who underachieve and those who are of low ability.
3. Planning includes opportunities for more able children to excel.
4. Advice is gained from specialists, particularly the SENCO.

Indicative forms of evidence

1. Use is made of test results, previous attainment, engagement with present work and deliberations between trainee and host teachers to ascertain pupil progress and potential.
2. Expectation for underachievers is set at a higher level than for those who are of low ability.
3. Tasks and activities are set at a conceptual level that makes appropriate demands of children who have been identified as more able.
4. Discussion with specialists about the attainment and attitude of individual children, including use of IEPs where appropriate, results in the establishment of targets for learning.

Specific forms of evidence

Accurate assessment...

Careful observation of children at work helps you to ascertain their attitude to learning. Scrutiny of test results gives you a perspective on children's capability under formal conditions. Careful analysis of the way that children go about the work offers insights into children's understanding and motivation. After conferencing with the host teachers, you reach decisions about planning and differentiating work such that the tasks and activities will be interesting and relevant to under-performing and less able children. For example, test results may indicate that a child is more capable than is evident in the way they deal with regular class work. Again, you may organise for learning such that children who distract one another are separated, resulting in higher achievement for both. Separation might also indicate which of two children that work together has the knowledge and understanding, and which one is the subordinate.

Distinguishing between underachievers and low ability...

Discussions that you have with individual children about their work and progress allows you to gain a fuller picture of their attitude to learning and subject preference. Your teaching includes a variety of closed questions that make knowledge demands of the children and more probing questions that require greater mental agility. The children's responses assist you in identifying those who have good memories (accurate answers to closed questions), those who can think laterally (thoughtful and unpredictable answers to open questions) and those who think slowly. Lesson plans are differentiated so that slower workers and less able children can engage meaningfully with relevant work that is sufficiently demanding to make them think but not simplistic.

More able children...

Your evaluations of children's achievements from test results, pupil profiles, observations, scrutiny of work and discussions with the children and teachers identify those children with exceptional capability. As a result, your planning and teaching caters for the children to have opportunity to explore alternatives, be creative and find solutions to problems. You ensure that the more able children are not left without purposeful work to do at an appropriate level for them and avoid excessively repetitive tasks.

Specialist advice...

You are able to provide the specialist teacher with the evidence that you have accumulated about the children who are not realising their full potential, discuss possible approaches to combat and improve the situation and implement the agreed strategies. You monitor the progress of the individuals and evaluate the impact of the strategies in written form or verbally with the specialist adviser and/or class teacher.

Comment

The factors that created an unsatisfactory situation with regard to the attainment of particular children were there before you arrived in the placement school and will still be there when you have left. You have a role in helping to provide a relevant and motivating curriculum for underachieving and low-attaining children, but as a student teacher your influence will only be partial. You can, however, help the class teacher and others concerned to provide a secure and purposeful learning environment so that the children have opportunity to find fulfilment in their work and make the best use of their time in school. In reality, this process is often slow and demanding. In more extreme cases it requires the active cooperation of parents and the involvement of the SENCO and/or the head teacher. Particularly for older primary age children, who have become entrenched in unsatisfactory ways of working or poor attitudes towards school generally, the task of stirring interest in academic work and convincing them that doing well is 'cool' needs a great deal of perseverance and ingenuity. Raising achievement often results from an amalgam of inner security, motivation and social acceptability. You must show that you have a grasp of these factors and can contribute towards improving a situation, but you are not expected to achieve in just a few weeks what the regular teachers struggle with regularly.

Standard

Trainees are able to support and identify the levels of attainment of those pupils who are learning English as an additional language, with the help of an experienced teacher where appropriate. Trainees can begin to analyse the language demands and learning activities in order to provide cognitive challenge as well as language support (S3.3.5, S3.2.5).

See QCA (2000) *A Language in Common: assessing English as an additional language.* Sudbury: QCA Publications.

Implications for practice

1. Assessment of competence in English through pupils' ability to comprehend through listening.
2. Assessment of competence in English through pupils' ability to comprehend through speaking.
3. Assessment of competence in English through pupils' ability to comprehend through reading.
4. Assessment of competence in English through pupils' ability to comprehend through writing.

Indicative forms of evidence

1. Pupils' responsiveness when hearing English spoken can be assessed with reference to the 'extended scale for listening' (QCA 2000, p. 12).
2. Pupils' ability to speak and use spoken English can be assessed with reference to the 'extended scale for speaking'.
3. Pupils' familiarity with the conventions of print and understanding written English can be assessed with reference to the 'extended scale for reading'.
4. Pupils' ability to write for different purposes can be assessed with reference to the 'extended scale for writing'.

Specific forms of evidence

Comprehension through listening…

You can distinguish between children who respond to spoken English in specific circumstances (e.g. a regular instruction such as 'please sit down'), those who can understand what is said but do not respond, and those children who can talk to others as a result of their understanding. You are familiar with the extended scale for listening (see below).

Spoken English...

You can distinguish between children who are able to say a few words, those who can sustain a conversation, and those who can modify their speech according to context and circumstances. You are familiar with the extended scale for speaking.

Reading English...

You can distinguish between children who are able to grasp basic written conventions, those who can read with support, and those who can read with a large degree of independence. You are familiar with the extended scale for reading.

Written English...

You can distinguish between children who are able to write English letters and their name, those who can use letter patterns, and those who can write recognisable letters, words and phrases. You are familiar with the extended scale for writing.

Comment

Assessment of English as an additional language in the areas of children's ability in listening, speaking, reading and writing are described with reference to a scale consisting of four stages for those who have yet to reach National Curriculum attainment target 1, namely:

- Step 1...for the least competent users
- Step 2
- Level 1, threshold
- Level 1, secure

Characteristics of each stage are described closely in QCA (2000), though some of the differences require fine judgement and are not wholly discrete. The scale for speaking and listening is separately listed for the four stages but combined for Level 2 and above. There are separate scales for reading and for writing. A variety of case studies are provided with descriptions of the contexts. You are advised to consult the document for complete details, especially pages 12–15. As with all assessments, however, the purpose of placing a child at a particular stage in the process is not for the sake of completing a record sheet and satisfying external requirements, but to clarify the child's progress to date and plan more effectively for the future. The nature of subsequent planning will depend upon a variety of factors, not least whether there are other children in the class with the same first language and the availability of a teaching assistant. It is also important to acknowledge the distress that a child experiences when suddenly thrust into a confusing new situation, with unfamiliar language, cultural norms and procedures. It takes time to induct any newcomer into fresh ways of working, and this problem is magnified for a child who speaks little or no English. Recording assessments might consist of an occasional summary paragraph about the child's abilities in speaking and listening, samples of written work as evidence for writing, and regular reading records for progress in reading. Assessment profiles of this kind should allow teachers to trace a child's curriculum experience in school and provide diagnostic information as a basis for discussing the child's progress with other staff and parents.

Standard

Trainees record pupils' progress and achievements systematically to provide evidence of the range of their work, progress and attainment over time and use this to help pupils review their own progress and inform planning (S3.2.6).

Implications for practice

1. Demonstrating an awareness of school records and recording systems.
2. Maintaining systematic records that inform planning and reporting.
3. Using information from records to set targets for learning for individual pupils.
4. Using information from records to assist planning.

Indicative forms of evidence

1. Ability to discuss with host teachers or tutors the range and use of records.
2. Contributions to the existing school record system or a parallel system.
3. Discussing work outcomes with pupils and agreeing the next stage in learning.
4. Using information from records to gain insights about appropriate lesson planning and differentiation of tasks.

Specific forms of evidence

Discussing range and use of records...

You show that you have looked at a sample of records and understand their purpose. You are able to interpret records and make constructive comments about their value and limitations.

Contributing to records...

You are able to maintain the existing class records for at least a sample of pupils to the satisfaction of the class teacher or mentor. Alternatively, you devise your own straightforward recording system that fulfils the same purpose. In either case, you have records available that can be accessed and understood by others.

Discussing outcomes...

You use information from formally maintained or informally written records about pupil progress and attainment as a basis for discussion with individual children or groups of children within a similar ability range to inform decisions about targets for learning.

Lesson planning...

You use records to guide you as to the appropriateness of learning objectives for different ability groups or individuals and make the link between records and planning obvious in written form (such as in a log or journal) or in conversations with a teacher or tutor.

Comment

Written records are not useful in themselves, but serve one or more of three purposes:

1. They provide detailed information that you cannot keep in your head.
2. They are a convenient means of passing on information to another adult.
3. They are a source of information to transfer to a formal record (such as a report).

Case study

Edwina was a conscientious trainee who was rightly proud of her excellent organisational skills and time management. Fellow students, teachers and tutors were all impressed with the meticulous way in which Edwina planned lessons (including assessment criteria) and maintained her file, and her perceptive insights that were reflected in daily evaluations of her teaching experiences and observations of experienced teachers. Edwina was the first to admit that her actual teaching did not always live up to the promise of her paperwork, but she was competent in the classroom and respected by staff and children for her integrity, enthusiasm and pleasant disposition. Edwina's one major concern, however, was about record-keeping. She had initially tried to keep records on every child in the class of thirty Year 2 children in core subjects but found it almost impossible to maintain them other than at a superficial level. After discussing the situation with her tutor she selected a 'sample' child from each of the six ability groups and kept a record that showed what curriculum content had been covered and how the children had coped with the tasks and activities. She intended to use the sample details as representative of the group as a whole but found that individual differences, even within a single group, were so marked that the curriculum 'coverage' approach was manageable but the 'achievement' element was far too general to be of much use in setting specific learning targets. After further discussion with the class teacher, she found that he claimed to keep a lot of information 'between my ears' (as he put it) and only wrote down specific entries when it was a quantitative score (such as the results of a spelling test). Edwina felt that she was not at the point where she could rely on memory to the same extent as the teacher, so she tried a compromise whereby she kept some quantitative scores and grades in maths and literacy and wrote a general comment about each child at the end of each week. Even this modest system proved extremely time-consuming to maintain. In addition there were reading records to oversee, though to her relief a teaching assistant took the main responsibility for them. By the end of her time on placement, Edwina had still not found a completely workable solution to keeping records and was anxious about the amount of effort that they took to complete, which detracted from lesson preparation. However, in her final meeting with the mentor a few days before she completed the placement, Edwina was commended for her intimate knowledge of the children's academic abilities and attainment. The mentor concluded that in grappling with the issue of keeping appropriate records, Edwina had subconsciously absorbed a considerable amount of information about the children's progress and potential, and utilised it in her planning and teaching. Edwina was pleased with the accolade but still uneasy about the prospect of maintaining records of children's progress and attainment for every child in the class when she had responsibility for a class of her own.

Standard

Trainees are able to use records as a basis for reporting on pupils' attainment and progress orally and in writing, concisely, informatively and accurately for parents, carers, other professionals and pupils (S3.2.7).

Implications for practice

1. Information from pupil records can be interpreted and understood sufficiently well to provide data for reporting to others.
2. Information about pupil progress can be explained to others.
3. Information about pupil progress can be presented in written form for the benefit of others.
4. Questions and queries from others about pupil progress can be answered satisfactorily.

Indicative forms of evidence

1. An understanding of reporting procedures used by schools and class teachers.
2. An ability to talk meaningfully about a pupil's progress to another adult.
3. The ability to communicate appropriate information about a pupil's progress accurately and clearly to another adult.
4. The ability to field questions and queries competently in such a way that knowledge about a pupil's progress is clarified and enriched.

Specific forms of evidence

Understanding of reporting procedures...

You can speak with confidence about reporting procedures after liaising with the class teacher or mentor, and after seeing a sample report.

Reporting verbally...

You have taken the opportunity to summarise the progress of at least one 'sample' pupil to the parent or to a surrogate (such as a teacher or assistant). In doing so, you conduct yourself with professional calm and speak with authority but sensitively and objectively.

Reporting in writing...

You have seen examples of written reports and discussed them with the teacher. You have taken the opportunity to summarise the progress of a sample of children in written form and shared the result with a teacher or tutor.

Fielding questions and queries...

You are able to respond to questions about a 'sample' child put to you by a parent or surrogate parent and provide specific information about the child, particularly relating to progress and attainment in core subjects, attitude to learning, social adjustment and potential. You demonstrate by your verbal summary and amplification of points in response to queries that you have collated accurate information about the child and can speak from an evidence base rather than relying on general impressions.

Conclusion

The job of teaching is complex and difficult. Like peeling off the layers of an onion, the more that you experience and understand, the more there remains to be experienced and understood! Teaching requires a lot of effort and perseverance, grappling with mistakes and errors, times of joy and moments of anguish, determination, release of self-confidence and an understanding of children and learning. Mastery of all these elements cannot take place in a hurry. *Try not to compare yourself with the class teacher who is probably a seasoned professional and has already trodden the path that you now follow.* Do your best to give a positive impression in school, maintain an open dialogue with teachers and tutors, show that you are determined to succeed and want to help children to do the same, and press forward boldly. Don't worry if you do not match all the high expectations described throughout this book. They present an *ideal* and need to be treated as such. Effective teaching involves more than complying with a set of individual criteria. It draws from intellectual and managerial skills, creativity, innovation, commitment and sheer energy (DfEE 1998b). You will not go far wrong if these descriptors are true of you.

Never lose sight of the impact that your teaching can have on the lives of the hundreds of children with whom you work. The old slogan that 'no-one forgets a good teacher' may be a little fanciful, but it is worth keeping in mind as you grind your way through the day. In the meantime, relish the privilege of influencing young minds and *enjoy your teaching.*

Bibliography

References

Arnold, R. (1990) 'Making the best use of teacher time', in Craig, I. (ed.) *Managing the Primary Classroom.* Harlow: Longman.

Brighouse, T. and Woods, D. (2003) *The Joy of Teaching.* London: RoutledgeFalmer.

Broadfoot, P. (1996) 'Do we really need to write it all down? Managing the challenge of national assessment at Key Stage 1 and Key Stage 2', in Croll, P. (ed.) *Teachers, Pupils and Primary Schooling.* London: Cassell.

Brown, G. and Wragg, E. C. (1993) *Explaining.* London: Routledge.

Carlyle, D. and Woods, P. (2002) *The Emotions of Teacher Stress.* Stoke-on-Trent: Trentham.

Carr, M. (2001) *Assessment in Early Childhood Settings.* London: Paul Chapman.

Clarke, S. (2001) *Unlocking Formative Assessment.* London: Hodder and Stoughton.

Clemson, D. and Clemson, W. (1996) *The Really Practical Guide to Primary Assessment.* Cheltenham: Stanley Thornes.

Cole, M. (ed.) (1999) *Professional Issues for Teachers and Student Teachers.* London: David Fulton Publishers.

Cole, M. (ed.) (2002) *Professional Values and Practice for Teachers and Student Teachers,* 2nd edn. London: David Fulton Publishers.

Collins, J. (1996) *The Quiet Child.* London: Cassell.

Cooper, P. and McIntyre, D. (1995) *Effective Teaching and Learning: Teachers' and Pupils' Perspectives.* Buckingham: Open University Press.

DfEE (1997) *Teaching: High Status, High Standards* (Circular 10/97). London: Teacher Training Agency Publications.

DfEE (1998a) *Induction for New Teachers.* Sudbury: DfEE Publications.

DfEE (1998b) *Teaching: High Status, High Standards; Requirements for Courses of Initial Teacher Training* (Circular 4/98). London: Teacher Training Agency Publications.

DfEE (2000a) *Curriculum Guidance for the Foundation Stage.* London: Department for Education and Employment.

DfEE (2000b) *Working with Teaching Assistants: A Good Practice Guide.* London: Department for Education and Employment.

DfEE/QCA (1999) The National Curriculum: Handbook for Primary teachers in England. London: Department for Education and Employment/Qualifications and Curriculum Authority.

DfES (2001) *Special Educational Needs Code of Practice.* Annesley: Department for Education and Skills.

DfES (2002) *Museum and Galleries Education Programme: A guide to Good Practice.* Annesley: Department for Education and Skills.

Drummond, M. J. (1993) *Assessing Children's Learning.* London: David Fulton Publishers.

Gipps, C., Brown, M. and McAlister, S. (1995) *Intuition or Evidence? Teachers and National Assessment of Seven-Year-Olds.* Buckingham: Open University Press.

Harding, J. and Meldon-Smith, L. (2000) *How to Make Observations and Assessments.* London: Hodder and Stoughton.

Hayes, D. (1999) *Foundations of Primary Teaching,* 2nd edn. London: David Fulton Publishers.

Hayes, D. (1998) *Effective Verbal Communication.* London: Hodder and Stoughton.

Hayes, L., Nikolic, V. and Cabaj, H. (2000) *Am I Teaching Well?* Exeter: Learning Matters.

Headington, R. (2000) *Monitoring, Assessing, Recording, Reporting and Accountability.* London: David Fulton Publishers.

Inman, S. and Buck, M. (1995) *Adding Value? Schools' Responsibility for Pupils' Personal Development.* Stoke-on-Trent: Trentham.

Jones, K. and Charlton, T. (eds) (1996) *Overcoming Learning and Behaviour Difficulties: Partnership with Pupils.* London: Routledge.

Kyriacou, C. (1991) *Essential Teaching Skills.* Cheltenham: Stanley Thornes.

Lindsay, G. and Desforges, M. (1998) *Baseline Assessment: Practice, Problems and Possibilities.* London: David Fulton Publishers.

Littledyke, M. and Huxford, L. (1998) *Teaching the Primary Curriculum for Constructive Learning.* London: David Fulton Publishers.

Mackinnon, C. (2002) *Teaching Strategies and Resources: A Practical Guide for Primary Teachers and Classroom Assistants.* London: David Fulton Publishers.

McNamara, S. and Moreton, G. (1997) *Understanding Differentiation.* London: David Fulton Publishers.

Merry, R. (1998) *Successful Children, Successful Teaching.* Buckingham: Open University Press.

Mitchell, C. and Koshy, V. (1995) *Effective Teacher Assessment: Looking at Children's Learning in the Primary Classroom,* 2nd edn. London: Hodder and Stoughton.

Noddings, N. (1992) *The Challenge to Care in Schools: An Alternative Approach to Education.* New York: Teachers' College Press.

Ofsted/DfEE (1996) *Setting Targets to Raise Standards: A Survey of Good Practice.* London: DfEE.

Ofsted (1995) *Homework in Primary and Secondary Schools.* London: HMSO.

Ofsted (2002) *The Curriculum in Successful Primary Schools.* London: Ofsted.

Pascal, C. and Bertram, T. (1997) *Effective Early Learning: Case Studies in Improvement.* London: Hodder and Stoughton.

QCA (1997) *The National Framework for Baseline Assessment: Criteria and Procedures for the Accreditation of Baseline Assessment Schemes.* London: Qualifications and Curriculum Authority.

QCA (1998) *The Baseline Assessment Information Pack.* London: Qualifications and Curriculum Authority.

QCA (2000) *A Language in Common: Assessing English as an additional language.* Sudbury: Qualifications and Curriculum Authority.

SCAA (1995) *Exemplification of Standards.* Sudbury: SCAA Publications.

SCAA (1997) *Desirable Outcomes for Children's Learning on Entering Compulsory Education.* London: HMSO.

Stern, J. (1995) *Learning to Teach.* London: David Fulton Publishers.

Suschitzky, W. and Chapman, J. (1998) *Valued Children, Informed Teaching.* Buckingham: Open University Press.

TTA (2002a) *Qualifying to Teach: Professional Standards for QTS and Requirements for Initial Teacher Training.* London: Teacher Training Agency.

TTA (2002b) *Handbook of Guidance on QTS Standards and ITT Requirements.* London: Teacher Training Agency.

Teare, B. (1997) *Effective Provision for Able and Talented Children.* Stafford: Network Educational Press.

Tymms, P. (1996) *Baseline Assessment and Value-Added: A Report to the Schools' Curriculum and Assessment Authority.* London: SCAA.

Wassermann, S. (1990) *Serious Players in the Primary Classroom: Empowering Children Through Active Learning Experiences.* NewYork: Teachers' College Press.

Winkley, D. (2002) *Handsworth Revolution: The Odyssey of a School.* London: Giles de la Mare Publishers.

Wragg, E. C. (1994) *An Introduction to Classroom Observation.* London: Routledge.

Websites

Commission for Racial Equality: www.cre.gov.uk/pubs

Department for Education and Skills (SEN): www.dfes.gov.uk/sen

National Grid for Learning (Inclusion): www.inclusion.ngfl.gov.uk
Qualifications and Curriculum Authority: www.qca.org.uk
Teacher Training Agency: www.canteach.gov.uk
Teaching Assistants: www.teachernet.gov.uk/teachingassistants_feedback_form

Further reading

Hayes, D. (forthcoming) *Foundations of Primary Teaching,* 3rd edn. London: David Fulton Publishers.

Index

David Fulton Publishers, The Chiswick Centre, 414 Chiswick High Road, London W4 5TF

Alternatively you can telephone, fax, email or order online:
Freecall: 0500 618052 Fax: 020 8996 3622
E-mail: orders@fultonpublishers.co.uk on-line: www.fultonpublishers.co.uk

ORDER FORM

Qty	ISBN	Title	Price	Subtotal
			p&p	
			Total	

Postage and packing: £2.50 for one or two books
Postage and packing is free for orders of three books or more.

Payment

☐ By credit card (Visa / Access / Mastercard / American Express / Switch / Delta)

☐ By cheque with order. Please make cheques payable to David Fulton Publishers Ltd.

☐ With invoice (applicable to schools, LEAs and other institutions)

Credit card number ☐☐☐☐☐☐☐☐☐☐☐☐☐☐☐☐☐☐☐

Expiry date ☐☐☐☐ valid from (Switch customers only) ☐☐☐☐ issue number ☐

Name	Order No./Ref
Position	Date
School/LEA/Company	
Address	
Telephone Number	Signature

☐